Marketing Management in Multinational Firms

Ulrich E. Wiechmann

The Praeger Special Studies program—
utilizing the most modern and efficient book
production techniques and a selective
worldwide distribution network—makes
available to the academic, government, and
business communities significant, timely
research in U.S. and international economic, social, and political development.

Marketing Management in Multinational Firms

The Consumer Packaged Goods Industry

Praeger Publishers   New York   Washington   London

PRAEGER SPECIAL STUDIES IN INTERNATIONAL ECONOMICS AND DEVELOPMENT

Library of Congress Cataloging in Publication Data

Wiechmann, Ulrich E
    Marketing management in multinational firms: the consumer
packaged goods industry.

    (Praeger special studies in international economics and
development)
    Bibliography: p.
    1. Marketing management.   2. International business
enterprises. I. Title.
HF5415.13.W53   1976   658.8   75-19831
ISBN 0-275-55850-9

PRAEGER PUBLISHERS
111 Fourth Avenue, New York, N.Y. 10003, U.S.A.

Published in the United States of America in 1976
by Praeger Publishers, Inc.

Printed in the United States of America

The years since World War II have seen unprecedented growth
in the international activities of both U. S. and foreign corporations.
With this expansion and, more especially, with the growth of direct
investment abroad the question of how to manage geographically
dispersed operations has become more and more pressing. The
answers to this question vary greatly among individual companies—
even companies within a single industry.

Company A, for example, sells a broad line of consumer products,
which are closely related in terms of marketing and technological
know-how. The company operates in a great number of foreign
countries and derives roughly 50 percent of its total sales and profits
from abroad. It is organized by product divisions, and each product
division manager has profit responsibility for a given product group
wherever it is sold.

Company A's foreign subsidiaries are tightly controlled from
headquarters in all functional areas. Executives at headquarters
direct almost all marketing decisions. The physical characteristics
of the products, the brand names, the package designs, and pricing,
for example, are largely determined at headquarters. Although the
subsidiaries have some latitude in the creative expression of advertising messages, headquarters prescribes which advertising agencies
may be used and is heavily involved in determining the allocation of
advertising budgets among the various media. Distribution decisions
are left mostly to the subsidiaries, but they receive recommendations
from a special advisory group for distribution analysis at headquarters.
Market research decisions are tightly centralized in Company A. All
market research plans must be approved by headquarters, which
determines the type of research, its scope, objectives, and methodology, and the research institute, if any, to be used.

Company A's marketing program for any given product shows a
great degree of uniformity from one country to another. One executive explained "We try to be as uniform and international as possible
and as different and national as necessary."

Company B has a product line that is very similar to Company A's.
Company B, however, derives only about 25 percent of its total
sales and profits from foreign operations. It is organized by geographical divisions, rather than product divisions, and each division
manager is responsible for all of Company B's products in his
particular geographical area.

"Our policy is to leave each subsidiary to develop and manage
its own business in conformance with some basic business principles

v

and to give a minimum of direction, " one executive at Company B headquarters observed. "These principles are not written down but learned and experienced as our men move up in the organization. We grow our own people, they come here after school and spend about 15 years with us before they become subsidiary general managers. At that time, they know what they can do and what they are supposed to do." Headquarters exercises relatively little direct control over subsidiary activities in the individual functional areas. Once the annual budget has been approved, the subsidiary manager has considerable freedom to act. Most decisions regarding product policy, advertising and promotion, pricing, distribution, and market research are made locally.

The differences in the management philosophy and practices of these two companies, both in the consumer packaged goods industry, raise two basic questions for multinational marketing management. First, what roles do executives at headquarters and executives in the subsidiaries play in managing the marketing function? Second, what is the importance of standardizing marketing programs from country to country?

These broad questions frame the scope of the issues to which this study addresses itself. Chapter 1 identifies major characteristics and management problems of multinational enterprises; it also states the research issues and objectives, establishes a model for research, and explains the research methodology employed. The next four chapters present the findings of field research conducted in U. S. -and Europe-based multinational enterprises. The relation between headquarters and the subsidiaries in marketing management is explored in Chapters 2 through 4, while Chapter 5 deals with the standardization of marketing programs. Chapter 6 summarizes the study's findings and presents some normative conclusions for management.

ACKNOWLEDGMENTS

This book has benefited from the inputs of many people and organizations, only a few of which can be mentioned here.

My deep gratitude goes to a group of individuals who—for reasons of confidentiality—must remain anonymous: the executives of the multinational enterprises that participated in this study. They gave many hours of their valuable time to answering and shaping my questions. Without the generous cooperation of these executives, this book could not have been written.

The study evolved out of a broader research project on multinational marketing initiated by my colleague, teacher, and friend Ralph Z. Sorenson II. His ingenuity, collaboration, and intellectual and moral support accompanied me in every phase of the study. The imprint of his contributions is present throughout the book.

I was fortunate to have easy access to the ideas, research skills, and experience of my colleagues Robert B. Stobaugh, Jr., and Steven H. Star. I am greatly indebted to them for their incisive and constructive criticism in the conceptualization and implementation of the study.

The final manuscript benefited significantly from the excellent editorial work of Gretchen Hovemeyer. She toiled hard to turn my notes into a readable document and relieved me of all the administrative burden involved in the preparation of the book for print.

CONTENTS

LIST OF TABLES

LIST OF CHARTS

Marketing Management in Multinational Firms

1

INTEGRATION: A KEY PROBLEM

The most conspicuous characteristic of any multinational enterprise is that it operates subsidiaries in a number of different nation states that often have vastly differing political, economic, and legal conditions.* Managing a multinational enterprise thus means managing a multiple-unit organization that must cope with a considerable degree of environmental diversity. A key problem for headquarters management of such an enterprise is how to tie together the business activities of the far-flung subsidiaries.

The diversity of the external environments in which the subsidiaries operate may make it necessary for them to follow substantially different business approaches. After all, an important function of any organization is to adapt to its external environment.[1] In addition, internal conditions of the individual subsidiaries, such as the views, objectives, and orientation of subsidiary managers, may show a considerable degree of diversity, increasing the propensity to follow a differentiated business approach from country to country.

---

*Multinational enterprise means any firm that conforms to the criteria established by Raymond Vernon in the Harvard Business School Multinational Enterprise Project, that is, any firm that at any one time has manufacturing subsidiaries in six or more countries and annual sales in excess of $100 million. See Raymond Vernon, Sovereignty at Bay: The Multinational Spread of U. S. Enterprises (New York: Basic Books, Inc., 1971), pp. 4-11.

The terms enterprise, firm, corporation, and company are used interchangeably in this study despite the distinctions that are sometimes drawn among them.

Existing side by side with the subsidiary's need to adapt its activities to these external and internal conditions, however, is the need of headquarters to integrate the activities of all subsidiaries. In the absence of such integration, that is, short of some unity and uniformity of foreign operations, the multinational enterprise would resemble a mere collection of diverse national companies. Integration is a key management task because it is the means of attaining the overall corporate objectives of the multinational firm and of best utilizing the firm's collective skills and resources.

Some efforts to integrate the operations of foreign subsidiaries will be found in any multinational enterprise. Differences will exist, however, in the extent to which integration is intended and accomplished. Moreover, both the integrative devices employed by various firms and the weight attached to them will differ. Finally, integration itself will appear in various forms, which will differ by firm and by business function. For the marketing function, a common form of integration is the standardization of marketing programs.

Major Integrative Devices

The integration of the foreign operations of a multinational enterprise does not occur automatically; it results from conscious efforts of headquarters management to influence the firm's subsidiaries to follow a uniform business pattern. The various modes of influence are called "integrative devices."[2]

An obvious way to influence the actions of a subsidiary manager is for headquarters management to exercise the hierarchical authority that it possesses. In other words, headquarters executives can impose decisions on subsidiary management by issuing orders and enforcing them at the operating level. This integrative device is called headquarters direction. It is the strongest and most direct manner of influencing the behavior of subsidiary managers, and is tantamount to a strict limitation of subsidiary autonomy.

Direction is, however, only one of several ways in which headquarters may influence subsidiary activities. Rather than by direct command, headquarters management of a multinational enterprise may try to achieve integration by establishing in each subsidiary manager the attitudes, organizational loyalties, and behavior patterns that will lead him to make only decisions that conform to headquarters intentions. Corporate acculturation is one term for this process. Herbert A. Simon calls it "internalization" of top management's influence, "because it injects into the very nervous systems of the organization members the criteria of decision that the organization wishes to employ."[3]

Corporate acculturation generally requires that subsidiary managers be selected carefully and trained extensively so that they will be ingrained with headquarters objectives and philosophy. Once they have been conditioned to follow a specific business approach, these managers will be able to run the firm's foreign subsidiaries with relatively little interference from headquarters. Antony Jay's illustrations in his historical analysis of corporate life are the Roman governor and the British colonial officer who ruled far from home with virtually no supervision or policy guidance. These men needed no guidance or control from home because they were "internally centralized" through years of indoctrination and training, which told them exactly what action they were to take. [4]

Headquarters direction and corporate acculturation stand at opposite extremes of the wide spectrum of integrative devices that may be used to influence the behavior of subsidiary management. Headquarters direction, broadly speaking, centralizes the decision-making power at the headquarters level, whereas corporate acculturation allows decentralized decision making at the subsidiary level. Between these extremes lie two other major integrative devices: systems transfer and personnel transfer. [5]

Systems transfer refers to the international transfer of formal communications, planning, and control systems. A multinational enterprise may be able to influence subsidiary managers to adopt uniform methods of solving business problems by insisting that they follow standard procedures for reporting and that they adhere to the same planning and budgeting exercises. The effectiveness of this integrative device may be enhanced by regularly disseminating to each subsidiary the experiences of subsidiaries in other parts of the world.

Personnel transfer refers to the establishment of personal contacts, across international borders, among headquarters and subsidiary managers. Personnel transfer can take the form either of short-term visits or of long-term assignments of managerial personnel in other countries. Personnel transfer helps not only to resolve differences in viewpoint among subsidiary managers which result from their differing external environments, but also to impress upon them the notion that each subsidiary is a part of a larger system and that each part must function in coordination with the others if the objectives of the whole are to be achieved.

The four integrative devices discussed here—headquarters direction, corporate acculturation, systems transfer, and personnel transfer—are only general categories that cover a broad range of specific individual integrative actions. Personnel transfer, for example, encompasses formal meetings of special integrating teams composed of headquarters executives and subsidiary managers as well as occasional visits by the headquarters marketing manager to

the firm's foreign subsidiaries. Moreover, the four devices involve
actions that are not mutually exclusive. To draw a clear line
between, for example, measures that enhance corporate acculturation and measures that enhance systems transfer is difficult. In
fact, insistence on common communications, planning, and control
systems (systems transfer) may be viewed as an important means
of attaining corporate acculturation.

Ultimate Objective of Integration

Whatever the integrative device or actions involved, a major
aim of headquarters is to provide its foreign subsidiaries with
inputs that will enable them to conduct their operations more successfully than their competitors. Headquarters possesses the accumulated
technological and managerial know-how from doing business in
different parts of the world which, combined with capital resources,
typically forms the basis for growth of the multinational enterprise. [6]
John Fayerweather has pointed out that the transfer of superior
skills from headquarters to foreign subsidiaries is crucial to the
survival of the multinational enterprise whose competitors are
other multinational enterprises and purely local firms. [7] In competing
against local firms the multinational enterprise starts with a number
of disadvantages: often a larger overhead, a limited knowledge of
local-market and -economic conditions, less favorable host-
government relations, plus the communications and control problems
associated with geographically dispersed operations. For a time,
foreign subsidiaries may be able to sustain the lower profit margins
that can result from these disadvantages and may be able to compete
successfully against local companies merely on the basis of the
multinational parent's greater financial strength. In the long run,
however, for a foreign subsidiary to maintain a competitive edge
over local enterprises requires that its skills and decision-making
powers be superior to what is available locally. [8] According to the
following statement by the chairmen of Unilever Limited and Unilever
N. V., the superior skills and the effective transfer of such skills
to subsidiaries is at the heart of multinational business. [9]

> The competitive advantages on which our success
> depends all rest in the last resort on knowledge.
> We have purely national competitors who can raise
> money at much the same price as we can, who are
> less heavily taxed, whose relative smallness makes
> speed of decision easier, who tend to be treated
> more benevolently by their own government, and for
> whom imitating the major international companies is

sometimes an effective substitute for research. What
they do not have is the immense body of varied knowledge and commercial skills which Unilever has built
up over the years.

The transfer of skills must be the ultimate objective of the
use of integrative devices. In fact, the entire process of integration
and the specific integrative devices mentioned above are in and of
themselves methods of transferring skills across borders. In the
case of headquarters direction, managerial know-how possessed by
headquarters is transferred to the subsidiaries in the form of decisions.
By contrast, the aim of both corporate acculturation and systems
transfer is to develop in each subsidiary manager the capability of
making appropriate decisions himself. Personnel transfer, finally,
takes specific skills of individuals within the organization across
international borders. Obviously, the method selected to integrate
foreign operations and to transfer skills will have a significant
impact on the relations between headquarters managers and subsidiary managers and on the relative roles that they play in managing
the multinational business.

SCOPE OF THE STUDY

Issues and Objectives

Discussions about the appropriate roles of headquarters and
subsidiary managers in decision making have occupied both businessmen and theorists for quite some time and have been particularly
heated in the marketing field. Views diverge widely on the degree
of autonomy which should be given to the personnel of foreign
subsidiaries and the extent to which headquarters should become
involved in making local marketing decisions.

Underlying these differing viewpoints are certain basic premises
about the nature of consumers around the world and about the
transferability of marketing know-how from country to country. Some
have argued, on the one hand, that consumer needs are basically
the same worldwide and that a multinational enterprise could therefore save considerably by centralizing marketing decisions at
headquarters and by transferring a uniform marketing approach to
each country.[10] Developing and enforcing a standardized marketing
program could be an effective method of transferring marketing skills.
On the other hand, others have emphasized the obvious dissimilarities among country markets, especially the markets for consumer
goods, and therefore support decentralization of the marketing
function.[11]

The headquarters marketing manager in a multinational enterprise clearly faces a dilemma. Greater headquarters control over marketing activities at the subsidiary level may be desirable as a means of achieving better integration and of making the best use of the company's international experience and marketing strength, yet the necessity of responding quickly and effectively to local market conditions may require that considerable freedom to act be available to subsidiary managers.

No one solution to this dilemma will be appropriate for every multinational enterprise. Hopefully, however, the present study can contribute to a better understanding of the way in which multi-national enterprises try to influence the activities of their subsidiaries toward a common marketing approach.

Although the emphasis of this study was on field exploration of the marketing management process, a survey of company case histories[12] and of available literature on multinational marketing management[13] suggested certain initial propositions about the use of integrative devices and the standardization of marketing programs. These propositions are summarized in Chart 1 and may be stated as follows:

First, the degree to which headquarters direction and the other integrative devices are employed appears to be influenced by three sets of factors:

1. Corporate factors. Variables that pertain to the "personality" of a multinational enterprise, such as strategy, organizational structure and process, and management philosophy.

2. Subsidiary factors. Variables that pertain to individual subsidiaries of a multinational enterprise, such as the size of each subsidiary, the nationality of subsidiary managers, organization, and profitability.

3. Market factors. Variables in the market environment of the individual subsidiaries, such as economic, social, and legal conditions, the nature of competition, and the availability of advertising media.

Second, the different ways in which multinational firms employ headquarters direction and the other integrative devices produce differences in the form and the extent of integration. Standardization of marketing programs is a form of integration. The extent of stan-dardization is influenced significantly by the degree of headquarters direction. [14]

The scheme in Chart 1 serves as the overall research model for this study. The specific research objectives are to explore the degree of headquarters direction in marketing and the factors that influence it, to describe the use of the other integrative devices in multinational firms, and to determine the extent to which and

CHART 1

Integration of Multinational Marketing:
Key Variables

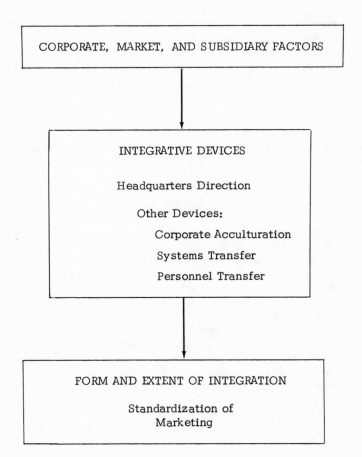

CORPORATE, MARKET, AND SUBSIDIARY FACTORS

INTEGRATIVE DEVICES

Headquarters Direction

Other Devices:

Corporate Acculturation

Systems Transfer

Personnel Transfer

FORM AND EXTENT OF INTEGRATION

Standardization of
Marketing

and the conditions under which headquarters exercises its authority
to standardize marketing programs across borders.

Of the three categories of factors shown in Chart 1 as variables
influencing the degree of headquarters direction, only corporate
factors are considered in detail. The basic premise for this restric-
tion is that each multinational enterprise tends to develop a general
pattern or policy of headquarters direction which is determined primarily
by corporate factors and which it attempts to apply to each of its
foreign subsidiaries. Prior research has provided some evidence
for the validity of this premise. [15]

Any multinational enterprise may occasionally need to modify
its general policy toward use of headquarters direction in order to
take account of specific subsidiary or market factors. In other
words, while corporate factors determine the basic level of headquarters direction in decision making, minor adjustments will be
made for individual subsidiaries in view of subsidiary and/or
market factors. Nevertheless, a reasonable step in attempting
to investigate the model in Chart 1 was to focus on the extent to
which corporate factors determine the general level of headquarters
direction.

Sample and Methodology

This study explores multinational enterprises selling non-
durable brand-name consumer products, specifically firms in the
food, soft drink, soap-detergent-toiletries, and cosmetics
industries. These firms were regarded as suitable for study for a
number of reasons.

These industries stand out as having spawned a substantial
number of major multinational enterprises.* A characteristic of
firms in these consumer packaged goods industries is that they
usually operate with fairly simple and mature product technology
and that they are in the top brackets of companies in all industries
in terms of advertising expenditures as a percentage of sales. [16]

In other words, consumer packaged goods firms seem to be
involved in a business in which marketing know-how, rather than
high technology, manufacturing scale economies, or financial
resources, is the key to success or failure. Presumably, therefore,
the consumer packaged goods firms are building their international

----

*See Raymond Vernon, op. cit., pp. 14-15. Of the 187
multinational firms that he identified from among Fortune's top
500 companies in the United States, 29 were in the SIC (Standard
Industry Classification) group "food and kindred products," and
another 25 were in the category "chemicals (minus drugs),"
which includes soaps, detergents, toiletries, and cosmetics.

strength primarily by transferring marketing skills across international
borders, in contrast to firms in other industries, many of which can
rely more heavily on technology transfer to develop an international
competitive advantage.

Although studies have been made of the international transfer
of technology by technology-intensive multinational firms, [17] little
empirical data exist so far on the degree to which marketing skills
have been transferred abroad by marketing-intensive multinational
firms or on the requisite management procedures or policy for such
transfer. [18] This scarcity is the principal reason for the type of
sample selected for study.

The research sample consisted of 27 multinational enterprises:
11 are in the food business, three sell soft drinks, nine are in the
soap-detergent-toiletries business, and four sell cosmetics. With
the exception of five European firms, all the companies in the sample
are headquartered in the United States.

Only the European operations of the participating firms were
investigated. This geographic limitation, which should be kept
in mind, seemed advisable because it would eliminate gross
differences in national market conditions (such as the country's
political system, national economic standard, infrastructure, and
level of education) which could affect company behavior so strongly
that discerning the relationship between the research variables
would be difficult.

In general, the cooperation of the sample companies was
excellent.* Information was gathered from roughly one hundred
persons, the respondents falling into two groups: 1. Senior
executives with marketing or general management responsibility
for Europe who were located at corporate headquarters or regional
headquarters for Europe, such as the president of an international
division or the vice-president in charge of marketing for Europe; and
2. Executives in local subsidiaries of 10 of the 27 companies, such
as the general manager and/or his marketing manager. The respon-
dent managers showed a high degree of interest in the study and
welcomed the opportunity to voice their views on the integrative
devices and on the standardization of marketing programs.

The study being aimed at gaining an understanding of the
"modus operandi" of the participating firms influenced the research
methodology in at least two ways. First of all, it became evident
very quickly that the necessary insights could not be obtained
through any technique other than personal interviewing. Although

----

*Occasionally not all 27 companies responded to a particular
question. Therefore, in some of the tables shown later, the number
of observations is less than 27.

the majority of the executives and firms were visited only once, a small core group of five companies was visited repeatedly to add more depth to the findings. The interviews were loosely structured by using a set of three personally administered guides or "questionnaires." These interview guides assured that the same kind of data was collected on each company, but they still allowed the respondents to mention the issues that they felt were the most pertinent. Of the two interview guides used at the headquarters level, one was aimed at obtaining general company data and was typically answered by the president of the international division or of the European head office. The other asked for product-specific information, which was usually supplied by product coordinators or headquarters executives in comparable positions. The third interview guide was administered at the subsidiary level. Many of the questions it contained were the same as those in the general interview guide used at the headquarters level, so that possible differences in viewpoint between headquarters and subsidiary management would be revealed.

Second, because the study focused on exploratory field research, the sample size and the number of observations for each variable were usually not large enough to permit statistically significant analysis. Hence, the findings and the conclusions presented in the following chapters are primarily based on the qualitative judgments and insights developed in the course of in-depth interviewing of the executives of the 27 sample firms. Yet certain information was gathered in a manner that allowed a modest amount of back-up quantification. Thus, the presentation of findings will blend the qualitative observations with some additional cues that emerged from the effort to quantify certain types of data.

NOTES

1. See Paul R. Lawrence and Jay W. Lorsch, Organization and Environment (Boston: Harvard University, Graduate School of Business Administration, Division of Research, 1967), pp. 6-11.

2. This discussion of the major integrative devices available to management relies largely on Herbert A. Simon, Administrative Behavior, 2d ed. (New York: The Free Press, 1965); and James G. March and Herbert A. Simon, Organizations (New York: John Wiley & Sons, Inc., 1958).

3. Herbert A. Simon, op. cit., p. 103.

4. See Antony Jay, Management and Machiavelli (New York: Holt, Rinehart & Winston, 1967), p. 66.

5. See, for example, Paul R. Lawrence and Jay W. Lorsch, op. cit., pp. 137-40.

6. See John Fayerweather, International Business Management: A Conceptual Framework (New York: McGraw-Hill Book Company, 1969), p. 136.

7. Ibid., pp. 171-72.

8. See ibid., p. 172.

9. Unilever Limited, Unilever's Role as a Multi-national Business (London: Unilever Limited, Information Division, 1972), pp. 4-5.

10. See, for example, Erik Elinder, "International Advertisers Must Devise Universal Ads," Advertising Age, November 27, 1961, pp. 91-96; Erik Elinder, "How International Can Advertising Be?" in S. Watson Dunn, ed., International Handbook of Advertising (New York: McGraw-Hill Book Company, 1964), pp. 59-71; Arthur C. Fatt, "The Danger of 'Local' International Advertising," Journal of Marketing, January 1967, pp. 60-62; Norman Heller, "How Pepsi-Cola Does It in 110 Countries," in John S. Wright and Jac L. Goldstucker, eds., New Ideas for Successful Marketing (Chicago: American Marketing Association, 1966), pp. 694-700.

11. See, for example, Millard H. Pryor, Jr., "Planning in a Worldwide Business," Harvard Business Review, January-February 1965, pp. 130-39.

12. See, for example, the Harvard Business School case studies: General Foods Corporation–International Division (D1) (Boston: Harvard University, Graduate School of Business Administration, 1964); General Foods Corporation–International Division (D2) (Boston: Harvard University, Graduate School of Business Administration, 1964); and Polaroid France (S. A.) (Boston: Harvard University, Graduate School of Business Administration, 1968).

13. See, for example, Robert J. Alsegg, Control Relationships Between American Corporations and Their European Subsidiaries (New York: American Management Association, Inc., 1971); Richard John Aylmer, Marketing Decisions in the Multinational Firm (doctoral dissertation, Harvard University, Graduate School of Business Administration, 1968); Michael Z. Brooke and H. Lee Remmers, The Strategy of Multinational Enterprise (New York: American Elsevier Publishing Company, Inc., 1970), Chs. 3 and 4.

14. See Aylmer, op. cit., pp. 196-97.

15. See C. Wickham Skinner, "Control in a Multinational Corporation," Worldwide P & I Planning, May-June 1967, pp. 24-32. Contrary to his initial expectations, Skinner found that multinational enterprises tended to use the same degree of command and involvement in decision making for all of their foreign subsidiaries. See also Alsegg, op. cit., p. 108.

16. See "Percentage of Sales Invested in Advertising in 1967-68," Advertising Age, January 25, 1971, pp. 77-78.

17. See, for example, W. H. Gruber, Dileep Mehta, and Raymond Vernon, "The R & D Factor in International Trade and International Investment of United States Industries, " Journal of Political Economy, February 1967, pp. 20-37; W. H. Gruber and D. G. Marquis, Factors in the Transfer of Technology (Cambridge, Mass.: M. I. T. Press, 1969); Raymond Vernon, ed. , The Technology Factor in International Trade (New York: Columbia University Press, 1970).

18. Two notable exceptions are Aylmer, op. cit. ; and Ralph Z. Sorenson, The Analysis of Competition Between Local and International Companies in Two Central American Industries (doctoral dissertation, Harvard University, Graduate School of Business Administration, 1967).

2

HEADQUARTERS DIRECTION AS
AN INTEGRATIVE DEVICE

DEFINITION AND MEASUREMENT

The term headquarters direction refers to the integrative device whereby the headquarters of a multinational enterprise uses hierarchical authority and direct orders to influence the decisions of its subsidiaries. Headquarters direction constitutes a limitation of subsidiary autonomy. Thus, the extent to which a foreign subsidiary is limited in determining the elements of its local marketing program indicates the degree of headquarters direction.

This study explores the extent to which authority for making marketing decisions rests with local subsidiary management or with some higher organizational level, without specifying what higher organizational level may be involved. In other words, whether marketing decisions are made at corporate headquarters or at regional headquarters is of much less concern here than whether marketing decisions are made at either of these higher organizational levels or by the local subsidiaries themselves. For this reason, the corporate hierarchy has generally been divided into just two levels: subsidiary management, on the one hand, and headquarters management, on the other, which may comprise more than one organizational level. Although interaction among different levels of headquarters management is not dealt with in depth, the manner in which the form of organizational structure above the subsidiary level may affect the degree of headquarters direction is investigated (see Chapter 3).

To measure the extent of headquarters direction, company managers were asked to rate, on a seven-point semantic differential scale, how much autonomy they thought the local subsidiaries had for each of a variety of marketing decisions, such as packaging, pricing, and advertising. Although this measure is clearly subjective, it was accepted because no objective criteria for determining the extent of headquarters direction could be identified. The possibility that executives at various organizational levels might have different perceptions of the degree of headquarters direction was explored initially by collecting the same type of information from more than one source within each company. Fortunately, those differences in perception which did exist between headquarters and subsidiary executives were generally found to be minor. Because of the confidence in the validity of the rating system as a whole which was thus gained, investigations in some companies could be confined to a single organizational level, usually regional headquarters.

To simplify presentation of the data, the interview responses on the seven-point scale that was used to measure the degree of headquarters direction were compressed into three ratings: high, moderate, and low. High stands for responses one, two, and three on the seven-point scale, low for responses five, six, and seven, and moderate for the midpoint response, four.

To speak of a high, moderate, or low degree of headquarters direction does, of course, conceal the often elaborate process of interaction, negotiation, and persuasion which usually takes place between headquarters and subsidiary management before important decisions are reached. Even in the most highly centralized companies that were investigated, decisions were very rarely made in complete isolation at headquarters and simply handed down to the subsidiaries for implementation without prior consultation. Decision making in multinational enterprises is invariably an interactive process involving several organizational levels. Thus, the ratings high, moderate, and low headquarters direction must be regarded as shorthand expressions for the extent to which headquarters exerts a predominant influence on the decision-making process.

An illustration of the interaction that takes place between headquarters and subsidiary management in decision making is presented by a major U. S. cosmetics company that introduced a new skin lotion both at home and in Europe. The product idea originated in Europe; product development took place in the company's central laboratories in the United States; packaging and basic advertising copy were developed at corporate headquarters; and the product was then presented to the European subsidiaries. Their reactions ranged from total rejection of the entire product idea, because of an alleged lack of local acceptance, to suggestions for changes in practically every dimension of the product, packaging, and advertising. Headquarters personnel discussed with each of the country managers the changes that would be necessary to meet local market conditions. Yet the overriding influence in the final

decisions was corporate management's philosophy that consumers'
attitudes toward the company's products were basically similar
around the world and that the company should develop and market
a uniform product line. The net result of headquarters-subsidiary
interaction was to change the product formulation only to meet
local legal requirements and to make a minor change in packaging
for the European market. Although the package used in Europe was
to be different from the one used in the United States, it was to
be identical in each of the European countries. The advertising
copy remained essentially the same except for modifications to
take account of language differences. In short, headquarters
exercised the predominant influence on marketing decisions, but
subsidiary management was actively involved in the process of
reaching those decisions.

HEADQUARTERS DIRECTION BY
BUSINESS FUNCTION

It has frequently been suggested that the extent of headquarters
direction of decision making is not identical for all business functions.[1] In particular, it has been stated that marketing—of all
functions—would be or should be the least headquarters-directed
because of the need to respond to differences and changes in
local market conditions.[2]

To see how marketing compared with other business functions,
company executives were asked to judge the degree of headquarters
direction involved in each of the following functions: finance,
manufacturing, research and development, purchasing, marketing,
and personnel. Their responses are summarized in Table 1.

Finance is the function that the executives of the vast majority
of the sample companies felt was controlled rigidly from headquarters.* The annual budget routine is but one means of exercising
financial control; detailed reporting on a monthly, a biweekly, or
even a weekly basis of key financial data is common. Control is
facilitated by the use of standardized accounting procedures. All

---

*This finding agrees with the results of a detailed investigation
of the financial control practices of multinational enterprises;
see Edward C. Bursk et al., Financial Control of Multinational
Operations (New York: Financial Executives Research Foundation,
1971), pp. 29-30. Two thirds of the 98 multinational companies
in Bursk's study exercised tight financial control of their subsidiaries; only 6 percent employed what they considered to be
loose control.

TABLE 1

Degree of Headquarters Direction by Business Function

Function	Degree of Headquarters Direction					
	High		Moderate		Low	
	Number	Percent	Number	Percent	Number	Percent
Finance	22	85	3	11	1	4
Manufacturing	11	42	7	27	8	31
Research and Development	18	69	3	12	5	19
Purchasing	4	15	3	12	19	73
Marketing	12	46	8	31	6	23
Personnel	11	42	6	23	9	35

but one of the sampled companies reported that the financial
accounting methods used by the subsidiaries are rigorously pre-
scribed by headquarters.

Decisions concerning research and development are also
tightly centralized in most companies. The reason is quite
understandable. Since research results can in most cases be
transferred easily from country to country, decentralized research
would often result in an unnecessary duplication of effort. Most
of the companies in the sample concentrated their research facilities
in one country, usually the home country. Those subsidiaries
which had their own separate research facilities confined their
activity mostly to adapting company products in minor ways to
meet local needs.

Two aspects of the manufacturing process—product specifications and product quality—tend to receive a great deal of headquarters
direction in most of the sampled companies. The major reason for
this tendency is that headquarters wants to ensure that products
carrying the company name meet established standards. One
headquarters executive said

> We exercise tight control over the manufacturing process
> in all our subsidiaries. We receive a daily laboratory
> report from each factory. Samples of every product that
> is manufactured overseas are sent to New York for evalua-
> tion.

Control is particularly important to companies with international
brands. If a common trademark is used in several countries, the
company will aspire to uniformity in product quality.

In terms of personnel decisions, the majority of the firms
examined showed a high or moderate degree of headquarters
direction. Virtually all of the companies, even those reporting
a low general level of headquarters direction for personnel decisions,
exert a strong influence from headquarters on the hiring and firing
of key subsidiary executives. The nature and the degree of headquarters involvement vary, however, from company to company.
Typically, headquarters management selects the subsidiary's
general manager and reserves at least a veto power over all
decisions concerning executives who report directly to the general
manager, such as the marketing manager and the financial manager.
Below these levels, headquarters influence on the selection and
dismissal of personnel is typically sporadic and only advisory in
nature.

Little influence is exerted by the headquarters of most of the
sampled companies on purchasing decisions—decisions about the
procurement of raw materials and supplies for manufacturing the

company's products. Headquarters direction in this area is usually confined to specifying the general level of quality of the ingredients used in manufacturing.

Marketing is by no means a function that headquarters typically leaves to subsidiary management. Almost half of the sampled firms reported a high degree, and almost another third a moderate degree, of headquarters direction in marketing decision making. Moreover, the interviews conveyed the impression of a trend toward increasing headquarters direction. Most of the executives—both at headquarters and in the subsidiaries—predicted that headquarters influence on marketing decisions would grow in the future. The following comments are representative:

> We are moving in the direction of more centralized decisions within the next two or three years.
>
> *   *   *
>
> There is currently a trend toward stronger centralization. The whole idea of setting up the regional office was to exercise control and coordination. We think it's more efficient to have some highly qualified senior guys here at headquarters who get more and more involved in subsidiary operations than to duplicate management skills at the country level. It's a way of life for us now and the subsidiaries are accepting it more and more.

In several firms, this trend was met with apprehension and objections at the subsidiary level. Subsidiary executives resisted the limitation of their autonomy and questioned the competence of headquarters to direct local marketing efforts. "What do they know up there about our problems?" was a comment frequently heard in this context. The resistance to growing headquarters direction was particularly pronounced in those firms which had given subsidiary management a free rein for many years. The vice-president international of one company described the situation as follows:

> I am suffering from the sins of omission made in the past. For years and years there was no global strategy, and as a consequence, we are now something different in almost every European country. Our overseas affiliates were left virtually independent and prospered on their own initiative. Some are still headed today by the same men who originally built them—often with great personal sacrifices—and who, by and large, have been very successful. It's a tough job to convince them of the virtues of a unified strategy. How do you

change somebody who is successful? We know we
have to reach a uniform image, but we have to do it
slowly. We can't move too fast if we don't want to
lose the motivation of the men overseas.

A major reason for the trend toward greater headquarters direction
of marketing decision making appears to be a growing awareness
among the sampled firms of the need and the opportunity for global
or regional planning rather than country-by-country planning. This
development is probably particularly pronounced in Europe. The
removal of trade barriers there, the growing mobility of consumers,
and the diminishing cultural differences among countries facilitate
the pursuit of a multinational marketing strategy with strong involvement of headquarters.

HEADQUARTERS DIRECTION BY
MARKETING DECISION

In rating the degree of headquarters direction involved in each
broad business function, several of the executives pointed out
that their responses did not reflect the complexity of the decision-
making process. One executive said:

Precisely how responsibility for a subsidiary company
is divided or shared between the head office and the
market head is a question to which a single and complete
answer cannot be given. The process is much more
complicated. One must further dissect a given functional
area into its component parts.

In line with this idea of further dissection, the managers of the
sampled companies were asked to examine their marketing programs
and to judge the degree of headquarters direction exerted on various
types of marketing decisions.
    For the purpose of this more detailed inquiry, the decisions
that must be made in establishing a marketing program were
divided into five general groups: (1) product policy decisions,
(2) pricing decisions, (3) advertising and promotion decisions,
(4) distribution decisions, and (5) market research decisions.
In addition, the specific elements of the marketing program which
each of these groups encompasses were defined.

1. Product policy decisions: Physical characteristics of the product;
    product line; brand name; packaging.

2. Pricing decisions: Suggested retail list price; trade margins.
3. Advertising and promotion decisions: Basic advertising message; creative expression of the message; sales promotion used for the product; allocation of advertising budget to different media; percent of sales spent on media advertising; percent of sales spent on sales promotion.
4. Distribution decisions: Type of sales force used; role of sales force in selling the product; manner in which the sales force is managed; percent of sales spent on sales force; distribution channels used (wholesalers, retailers); role assigned to middlemen in selling the product; type of retail outlets used to sell the product; percent of retail outlets covered.
5. Market research decisions: Type of market research studies conducted; percent of sales spent on market research.

Ratings were obtained on semantic differential scales for each one of these individual marketing program elements. In addition, the company executives were asked to provide ratings for the five broad groups of decisions involved in establishing their marketing programs. The results of this detailed investigation into the degree of headquarters direction exerted on marketing decisions are presented in the sections that follow. Tables 2 and 3 summarize the quantitative data and provide an overview of the variation in the extent of headquarters direction of the marketing function.

Product Policy Decisions

In discussions with company executives, decisions concerning the firm's product line, the physical characteristics of products, brand names, and packaging appeared to involve more headquarters direction than any other types of marketing decisions. This impression was confirmed by the generally high ratings that the executives gave on the semantic differential scale to quantify their judgments of the strength of headquarters control in the product policy area (see Tables 2 and 3). The finding of a high degree of headquarters direction for product policy decisions also accords with the results of earlier research.*

----

*See, for example, E. R. Barlow, Management of Foreign Manufacturing Subsidiaries (Boston: Harvard University, Graduate School of Business Administration, Division of Research, 1953), p. 109. He observed close headquarters control over product line additions, product eliminations, and product quality in all of the multinational companies he investigated.

TABLE 2

Degree of Headquarters Direction by Marketing Decision

Marketing Decision	High		Moderate		Low	
	Number	Percent	Number	Percent	Number	Percent
Product characteristics	18	86	2	9	1	5
Brand name	18	86	2	9	1	5
Packaging	18	86	3	14	0	0
Product line	19	90	0	0	2	10
Retail price	6	29	4	19	11	52
Trade margin	3	14	5	24	13	62
Basic advertising message	8	38	5	24	8	38
Creative expression	7	33	4	19	10	48
Sales promotion	2	9	6	29	13	62
Media allocation	3	14	4	19	14	67
Percent of sales spent on advertising	14	70	3	15	3	15
Percent of sales spent on sales promotion	11	55	6	30	3	15
Type of sales force	7	33	2	10	12	57
Role of sales force	3	14	5	24	13	62
Management of sales force	3	14	3	14	15	72
Percent of sales spent on sales force	14	67	1	5	6	28
Distribution channels	4	19	5	24	12	57
Role of middlemen	4	19	4	19	13	62
Type of retail outlets	5	24	4	19	12	57
Percent of outlets covered	9	43	3	14	9	43
Type of market research	5	24	3	14	13	62
Percent of sales spent on market research	11	52	5	24	5	24

TABLE 3

Degree of Headquarters Direction by Group
of Marketing Decisions

| Decision Group | Degree of Headquarters Direction | | | | | |
| | High | | Moderate | | Low | |
	Number	Percent	Number	Percent	Number	Percent
Product Policy	17	85	3	15	0	0
Pricing	5	25	7	35	8	40
Advertising and Promotion	8	40	8	40	4	20
Distribution	7	35	2	10	11	55
Market Research	5	25	3	15	12	60

22

The executives of the sampled companies agreed that ideas for new products or for product modifications may come from any part of the company, but before any such ideas can be implemented, at least headquarters approval is required. One headquarters executive said:

Products may be initiated at the local level, but I approve and I am informed and involved from day one.

In most of the companies, however, headquarters does not confine its role to evaluating and approving proposals coming from the subsidiaries. More typically, headquarters plays the dominant role in product concept definition, in the formulation of physical characteristics, packaging, and labels, and in product positioning. An extreme case of headquarters domination of these decisions is illustrated by the following excerpt from a company memorandum:

the intention in International markets will be to launch effectively and profitably all new products as they come from [headquarters], as far as practicable in the identical form and packaging.

It is appreciated that there will be cases where it is practical and necessary to deviate from [headquarters] standards. Any such deviation will be properly documented by the [subsidiary] and submitted to [headquarters] in recommendation form.

Among the individual elements of product policy, the brand name of a product was rated as particularly high in headquarters direction. The establishment of an international brand name for a given product is generally regarded as an essential source of competitive strength by companies in the consumer goods field. Strong headquarters control over brand-name decisions is exercised to protect the asset that an established international brand name represents and to coordinate the activities connected with the establishment of new international brands.

The problems that companies encounter in establishing international brand names are often formidable. National trademark laws and the legal rights of existing local brands, for example, can create major obstacles to devising an international brand name. In several European countries, any company can register a brand name with the patent office and thereby prevent a competitor from using the same name, even if the name is never used after its registration. One executive related that an important addition to the firm's product line had been considerably delayed because of the difficulty of finding an acceptable brand name that could be

legally used and protected in all of the firm's European markets.
Another obstacle to the creation of an international brand name is
the connotation a consumer might attach to a certain name. One
company had to modify the name for its pet food from "Friskies" to
"Friskis" in Germany because pretests of the first spelling had
shown that consumers associated it with the German words "friss
Kies," which mean "eat sand." The subsequent change in spelling
changed the pronunciation and greatly reduced the negative connotation.

The use of an international brand name for a product is usually
coupled with strong headquarters direction of other product policy
decisions. A firm that uses an international brand name typically
endeavors to achieve the greatest possible uniformity of product
quality, image, and appearance. Thus, the prescriptions by
headquarters of product characteristics and package design are
mandatory. An executive in a company that consciously pursues the
idea of using an international brand name, rather than numerous
local brand names, commented

> Brand policy, label policy, and packaging policy are
> all dealt with together at headquarters . . . here
> and there we have let a few markets run away with
> their own ideas in the past. But the present trend . . .
> goes definitely toward a much stricter application of
> the basic policy.

To implement its policy, the company maintains a large packaging
and labeling department at headquarters for design work. Once a
new logotype, label, or package has been designed, international
prototypes and precise instructions are sent out to all the company's
subsidiaries.

Although headquarters direction of product policy decisions
is generally high among the firms sampled, some differences appear
to exist among industries. These differences were revealed by
comments the executives made to explain their ratings. Executives
in three out of the four cosmetics firms and in all of the soft drink
firms indicated that headquarters control was extremely tight, very
little flexibility being left to the subsidiaries. A headquarters
executive in one of the cosmetics companies said

> We have taken the major marketing decisions away
> from the field and centralized them in New York.
> Everything is developed in New York: the products,
> the name, the package, the creative work, the
> display material, the whole marketing mix. Our
> basic philosophy looms over the heads of all country
> managers.

In contrast, the executives of the food firms explained that subsidiary management tends to have a strong influence on product policy decisions. These executives believe that foods require more adaptation to local consumer tastes than other products and that subsidiary management must therefore have the authority to change product specifications. Even in the food companies that subscribe to this point of view, however, subsidiary management must generally consult headquarters and obtain approval of its product policy decisions.

Pricing Decisions

Pricing decisions have the most direct impact on a firm's revenue and profitability. As Stefan H. Robock and Kenneth Simmonds have pointed out,[3] pricing is also an area in which the interests of various parts of a multinational enterprise may conflict. Each subsidiary manager may prefer prices that will contribute to his subsidiary's profitability and eliminate transshipments into its market from other countries; the vice-president international may favor prices that maximize total divisional profits; and legal counsel may worry about the antitrust implications of price decisions.

Pricing being so important to so many different parts of a multinational enterprise, it would presumably be closely controlled from headquarters. The company interviews indicate, however, that subsidiary autonomy in pricing decisions is generally high. The typical response of the executives interviewed was that decisions on retail prices, wholesale prices, and trade margins are "purely local." This response is reflected in the large number of low and moderate ratings given by these executives on the semantic differential scale for headquarters direction of pricing decisions (Tables 2 and 3). A high degree of subsidiary autonomy in pricing is deemed necessary to meet differences and changes in local market conditions.

> Prices cannot be dictated from the central office. The countries are too different. Manufacturing costs, competitors' prices, taxes all vary from country to country. So, the situation in the local market is a critical factor for pricing decisions.

In view of the differences in local market conditions, any attempt to direct pricing from headquarters—perhaps even for multiple products with short life cycles—is burdensome from an administrative standpoint. Moreover, it can endanger the subsidiaries' ability to react swiftly to competitive price moves. Consequently, in most of the companies visited, headquarters management was satisfied with a general discussion of pricing during budget meetings and with being informed, on a regular basis, of price changes that were made by the subsidiaries.

Even in firms whose headquarters exercised very tight control over most other marketing decisions the subsidiaries tended to have relatively great latitude in setting prices. The executives of all of the three highly centralized cosmetics firms mentioned this tendency. In these firms, headquarters put some constraints on subsidiary autonomy, however, by giving guidelines such as the following:

> [Our] products should command a premium price, although not necessarily the top price in the market, and therefore should appeal to the consumer to whom superiority . . . [is] important.

To headquarters management, these guidelines are very important in ensuring uniform positioning of the firm's products, relative to competition, in all markets, but they also leave subsidiary management free to determine actual prices.

Advertising and Promotion Decisions

Headquarters direction of advertising and promotion decisions showed the greatest variation from one industry to another. Within this group of decisions, the ratings obtained on the basic advertising message and its creative expression differed the most by industry.

All but one of the four companies in the cosmetics industry were at the extreme of very tight headquarters direction of the general advertising theme, its creative expression, the copy layout, and text. All of these elements are determined at headquarters, with little consultation of subsidiary management, and a complete advertising plan covering a six-month period is presented to subsidiary management at biannual meetings. During these meetings, criticism of the plan is welcomed, but major changes are rarely made. The subsidiaries are provided with sample advertising copy for each product, together with detailed directions for its reproduction and specific instructions not to change it. The following instructions typically go to each subsidiary along with complete advertising copy and layout:

CREATIVE CONCEPT
. . . strictly for the young individualist. The colors come in this fall's new rich, moody shades, in eye, cheek and lip makeup.

The target consumer is the up-to-date young w
aged 18-24. Copy talks to her directly, appealing
her inventiveness in making up her face. The visu
shows the effect that she can achieve by experimer
. . . .

MECHANICAL DIRECTION

MAIN ILLUSTRATION: [11 x 14 Ektachrome] View on
500K Macbeth Viewer. This illustration has sharp
definition of light and color and this mood should be
retained in engraving. Do not, however, go any stronger
in color in the dark areas than is shown in art. Retain
glisten on bottom lip. Crop illustration as layout . . . .
TYPE: Headline and signature Kabel Bold. Body copy
is Kabel Light. All type surprints in black.
PLEASE DO NOT DEVIATE FROM THIS LAYOUT. HOWEVER,
IF IT IS ESSENTIAL TO DO SO, PLEASE REMEMBER TO
SUBMIT COPY AND LAYOUT TO . . . FOR . . . APPROVAL.

The major reason for the high degree of headquarters direction
in the cosmetics industry is the conscious effort of most firms to
project a uniform company and product image in all countries. One
headquarters executive remarked

We are aiming at a worldwide look. Our strategy is:
uniformity and deviations only where absolutely necessary. That requires some benevolent dictatorship in
dealing with our overseas branches. We use an iron
fist with a velvet glove.

To justify using a high degree of headquarters direction and a uniform
marketing approach around the world, most executives maintained
that consumer interests for cosmetics were quite similar from country
to country. Consequently, they regarded the delegation of decision-
making power for local campaign adaptation as mostly unnecessary,
uneconomical, and potentially detrimental to the overall company
image. The following comments from high-ranking executives in
three different cosmetics companies underscore this point:

When it comes to cosmetics, women all over the world
are basically the same.
        *   *   *
. . . women's basic attitudes to beauty and beauty
products are similar the world over.
        *   *   *
A woman is a woman is a woman, irrespective of where
she lives . . . . Even in Japan we use the same copy,
with American models and English words.

The soft drink companies in the sample directed advertising decisions from headquarters but left subsidiary management with somewhat greater flexibility than did the cosmetics firms. In two of the three soft drink firms, the following approach was used: headquarters developed a prototypic advertising campaign that was disseminated to the individual subsidiaries with the expectation that they would adopt the basic advertising message. The president of the regional headquarters of a major soft drink company commented

> Whenever any subsidiary manager wants to depart signifi-
> cantly from our worldwide strategy he better have some
> very sound reasons, backed up by evidence for doing so.

Subsidiaries of soft drink companies were given a high degree of autonomy for the creative expression of the basic advertising message. For example, one executive related that the advertising slogan emanating from headquarters could not be translated meaningfully into the local languages of several subsidiaries. In addition, the advertising copy depicting social gatherings looked foreign in several markets. Both slogan and copy were adapted to local conditions, but were kept in line with the main thrust of the model campaign developed at headquarters.

In the food industry, subsidiary management apparently takes a much more active and authoritative role in promotional decision making. Most of the executives interviewed felt that advertising campaigns for food products require a great amount of custom tailoring because of country-to-country differences in such factors as consumer tastes and product-use patterns. Any attempt to direct this custom tailoring from headquarters would be administratively burdensome. The following excerpts from a presentation made by the product manager for freeze-dried coffee in one of the sampled firms illustrates this point.

> There are considerable variations in consumption per
> head . . . . The Scandinavians consume between 10
> and 11 kg of coffee per person and consider coffee to
> be a way of life. So it is not surprising that our
> message should be different in Sweden compared to
> the U. K. where coffee consumption is less than one
> third as high. . . . Unlike Coca-Cola, almost every
> market has its own coffee blend to match taste and
> hence the terminology has to be different . . . .
> Also one must consider the almost religious signifi-
> cance which coffee has in some markets where its
> preparation and drinking are intimately connected
> to the family and social scene . . . .

Thus, systematic international analysis indicates
that we are working under varying market conditions
which lead to different specific local marketing challenges.
The elements of the basic analysis are invariably the same—
but each factor varies in nature and importance from country
to country. The following advertisements show how the
end result differs internationally:

In Germany, our marketing analysis indicated that
our main objective . . . has been to build a premium
image and to remove the last vestiges of the ersatz
overtones that have been an obstacle to the development
of instant coffees in that country . . . .

Sweden: Since instant coffee has such a tiny share
of the coffee market . . . , our main objective is to get
the consumer's attention through interest-arresting
shock tactics. The message here is that a coffee cup
can be the world's least expensive coffee brewer . . . .
Notice that in this ad neither people nor the package
are shown.

The product manager's presentation for the remaining countries
showed that each market required a different advertising approach.
In the past, headquarters had tried to coordinate the various
country approaches and guide them toward greater uniformity.
Headquarters concluded, though, that the administrative headaches
connected with such direction were greater than any possible
advantages and that subsidiary management should therefore play
the decisive role in shaping local advertising programs.

For promotional decisions on elements other than the basic
advertising message and its creative expression, differences in
headquarters direction were less apparent from one industry to
another. Most companies allowed their subsidiaries considerable
autonomy in media selection and sales promotion. Decisions in
those areas, it was felt, were primarily dictated by local media
availability and local trade practices, which could not be adequately
monitored from headquarters. Decisions involving expenditure
levels—advertising and sales promotion budgets—tended, however,
to be closely controlled by headquarters. Like most other major
financial decisions, they had to be justified by subsidiary management during annual budget presentations. This tendency is reflected
in Table 2, which shows that a comparatively large number of firms
rated headquarters direction as high for decisions concerning
expenditures for advertising and promotion.

Tight headquarters control of advertising decision making is
occasionally accompanied by a prescription from headquarters of
the advertising agency that the subsidiaries must use. In the most

extreme case observed, the company employed the same advertising
agency around the world. The use of a single agency is in itself
an effective mechanism for controlling advertising decisions. The
vice-president international in one company said

> Using a single agency leads to a lot of worldwide coordi-
> nation of our advertising. The agency has one man who
> is specifically assigned to do this job for us. We get
> very much involved with them. We have never had the
> problem that a subsidiary wanted to go way out of line.
> If somebody did, we would hurry in immediately.

Less rigid than this single-agency approach is the procedure
that was observed in another firm: subsidiary managers could
choose among the four agencies nominated by headquarters. For
subsidiary management to use some other agency, however, required
headquarters approval. In general, agency prescription by headquarters tends to be the exception rather than the rule. Even in
some of the most centralized companies studied, many executives
took a pragmatic view of agency selection, as the following quotation
shows:

> We feel that the most talented and the most capable agency
> should handle our account in each country. If that happens
> to be an international agency we work with in a number
> of other countries, we don't object. But it may just as
> well be that a local agency is better equipped to do the
> job.

Distribution Decisions

Distribution decisions appeared to be an area in which headquarters executives typically do not get significantly involved.
Most of the managers interviewed spontaneously labeled these
decisions as "purely local." The major exceptions, again, were
decisions affecting the subsidiaries' spending levels, such as
the percentage of sales to be spent on the sales force (see Table 2);
such decisions had to be justified in annual budgetary discussions
with headquarters. The principal reason for giving subsidiaries a
large amount of autonomy in other distribution decisions was the
feeling at headquarters that the variations from country to country
in such factors as the type and number of outlets, the functions
performed by middlemen, and the relative importance of retail
institutions were too manifold to be handled from headquarters.

For example, among the European subsidiaries of one firm, direct sales to retailers as a percentage of total sales ranged from 80 percent in Belgium to zero in Sweden. This broad range is mainly a reflection of national differences in the role and relative importance of wholesalers, a factor over which the company had no control. Moreover, the breakdown of retail sales by type of outlet—such as supermarkets, drugstores, voluntary chains, and consumer cooperatives—varied greatly because of national differences in the structure of the distributive trade. Although headquarters might obtain a general picture of these country-to-country differences, it would be impossible, the executives felt, to monitor centrally the constant changes in distribution structure and to adjust local marketing programs to meet these changes through decision making at the top.

Although low headquarters direction of distribution decisions was the prevailing view, there were some exceptions. In one firm, management had created a central distribution research unit at headquarters. This unit compiled detailed data on the distribution conditions in each subsidiary market and conducted fairly sophisticated analyses for each subsidiary, such as profitability analyses by channels of distribution, minimum order size by type of outlet, and optimum call frequency for salesmen. The communications issued by this headquarters unit to the subsidiaries were characterized as "strong recommendations or guidelines," yet they did not preclude the participation of subsidiary management in decision making.

The headquarters of four other companies used less detailed, strategic guidelines, such as the following:

. . . [our] products should be sold on a selective basis to those outlets which can represent the company appropriately and effectively.

The objective of these general guidelines was to establish distribution networks of similar quality in each country which were consistent with the uniform image that headquarters wanted to project for the firm's products.

Market Research Decisions

In discussing the extent to which headquarters directs local market research decisions, one headquarters executive said: "Market research is a local decision; we don't watch it, but it has to be approved in the budget." This comment is representative of the attitude prevailing in the sampled firms, which is also reflected in their interview responses (see Tables 2 and 3). Market research decisions receive little headquarters influence. Often, the only headquarters involvement in market research decisions is a review of the size of the market research budget, which occurs during regular annual budget discussions. The subsidiaries then have complete freedom to allocate the budget to research projects as they see fit and to design such projects themselves.

The prevalence of this approach is surprising. It typically results in fragmentation of the company's total research effort, in duplication of research work, and in incomparability of market data from country to country, because of the differing market research methods chosen by the various subsidiaries. Fortunately, a growing number of headquarters executives are realizing that the absence of headquarters involvement in market research decisions limits the overall effectiveness of headquarters to integrate multi-national marketing operations. For this reason, several companies have created a position at headquarters called "market research director" to coordinate local market research efforts.

One of the firms visited has developed a set of very specific policies and procedures that force subsidiaries toward uniformity in market research. "Market research is the most centralized activity in the whole complex of marketing decisions," executives in this company stated. Before any market research is conducted, subsidiary and headquarters staff formulate the research objectives together. Subsidiary management then submits to headquarters a detailed research proposal that covers research objectives, the scope of the research project, the research methodology to be employed, and the research institute to be used. Headquarters evaluates the desirability of the project and its compatibility with the rest of the company's research activities, and then either approves the project, asks for modifications, or rejects it. Head-quarters executives of this firm argue that the strong involvement of headquarters in the market research process—though admittedly an administrative burden—lessens considerably the total research outlays of the company. More important, they feel that because the research results obtained are internationally comparable, headquarters management can better use the experiences gathered in one market for the solution of problems in another country market. Management regarded its policies and procedures for coordinated market research as an essential source of competitive strength.

It could be argued that this company may have pushed the idea of directing market research from headquarters to an extreme that might delay or even prevent the collection of important market information, and that such an extreme may be unnecessary. Another company reported that it achieved research coordination simply by developing marketing research guidebooks for all subsidiaries and by bringing subsidiary and headquarters market research personnel together for periodic conferences. The other extreme of no headquarters direction at all in market research decisions is far more questionable, however, if headquarters simultaneously pursues the policy of heavily directing other marketing decisions. Headquarters direction of marketing decision making, to be sensible, requires detailed knowledge about subsidiary markets and, consequently, involvement in market research decisions.

NOTES

1. See Michael Z. Brooke and H. Lee Remmers, The Strategy of Multinational Enterprise (New York: American Elsevier Publishing Company, Inc., 1970), p. 80; and Robert J. Alsegg, Control Relationships Between American Corporations and Their European Subsidiaries (New York: American Management Association, Inc., 1971), Chs. 5 and 6.

2. See, for example, Millard H. Pryor, Jr., "Planning in a Worldwide Business," Harvard Business Review, January-February 1965, pp. 130-39.

3. Stefan H. Robock and Kenneth Simmonds, International Business and Multinational Enterprises (Homewood, Ill.: Richard D. Irwin, Inc., 1973), pp. 461-62.

3

CORPORATE FACTORS INFLUENCING
HEADQUARTERS DIRECTION

One of the objectives of this study is to identify the corporate factors that influence the degree of headquarters direction of marketing decision making. [1] Broadly speaking, the degree of headquarters direction appears to be related primarily to characteristics of the firm's product line and to the management style of senior executives at headquarters. The characteristics of the product line include the degree of product diversification, the nature of the firm's products in relation to the culture of foreign countries, and the relative newness of products to the firm. These characteristics of the product line together with the management style of senior executives largely determine what headquarters practicably can do and what it wants to do in terms of central control. Two additional factors appear to affect the degree of headquarters direction: the existence of outsider influence as a result of foreign subsidiaries being formed through acquisitions and the extent of supply interdependence among subsidiaries, arising from the geographical concentration of production facilities.

Other factors studied were the organizational structure of the multinational enterprise and the relative importance of foreign operations to the firm. These factors, however, did not provide an explanation for variations in the degree of headquarters direction among the sampled firms.

The factors investigated are most likely not independent but, rather, collinearly related. Since the analysis in the following sections treats each corporate factor and the degree of headquarters direction as bivariate data, it does not give a complete picture of the strength of the relationship between the factors and headquarters direction. More sophisticated techniques of multivariate analysis would have been appropriate had the number of observations gathered in the field been greater.

CHARACTERISTICS OF THE PRODUCT LINE

Product Diversification

A key element of corporate strategy is the choice between a single-product concept and a multiple-product concept, that is, the degree of diversification of the product line. Prior research[2] has shown that the degree of diversification of the product line has a significant impact on how authority for decision making is divided among organizational subunits. Presumably, then, the degree of product diversification in a multinational enterprise will affect the role of headquarters and subsidiary management in decision making.

Leonard Wrigley established four categories indicating different degrees of product diversification: (1) single product, (2) dominant product, (3) related product, and (4) unrelated product. He sees these four categories as "lying along one single dimension through conceptualization of a product in terms of the core skill required in a firm for economic production in a competitive market."[3] He defines the core skill as "the collective knowledge, skills, habits of working together, as well as the collective experience of what the market and the technology will bear that is required in the cadre of managerial and technical personnel if the firm is to survive and grow in a competitive market." He characterizes firms falling into four categories as follows:[4]

1. Single product. Firms that rely on just one basic product and expand by simply increasing the volume within the area of one clearly defined core skill.

2. Dominant product. Firms 70 percent or more of whose output is accounted for by one product. They are similar to single-product firms except that they have added in a small way to their product line.

3. Related product. Firms that expand into new markets and/or use new technologies, but rely on an original core skill to ensure that each new product adds strength to the preexisting products, as well as drawing strength from them—as in common support of a research or marketing program.

4. Unrelated product. Firms that grow by expanding into new markets and new products and require a new core skill for each product, that is, a core skill that does not evolve from an original core skill. Conglomerates are typical of companies in this category.

Wrigley's research validated the proposition that the degree of divisional autonomy will be the greater the more diversified a company's product line is. Unrelated-product firms give more autonomy to their divisions than do related-product firms and much more than do dominant-product firms. The differences in divisional autonomy were observed to be particularly pronounced in the area of market decision making.

Supposedly, a similar relationship exists between the degree of diversification of a multinational enterprise in foreign markets and the degree of subsidiary autonomy in marketing decision making. The sampled companies are either dominant-product or related-product firms when classified by the nature of their product lines abroad. Since the distinction between related and unrelated products for firms relying on multiple products is therefore not needed, two categories have been used to distinguish the degree of product diversification: (1) dominant product, consistent with Wrigley's definition, and (2) multiple product, a more general term for Wrigley's related-product category.

The sample included five dominant-product firms, all of which gave the impression of being highly headquarters-directed. For example, in one of these firms, headquarters management met weekly to discuss the operations of the foreign subsidiaries. These weekly meetings were attended by the firm's president, executive vice-president, vice-president international, and, at times, even the chairman of the board. These meetings seemed to be the place where most decisions were really made; top management apparently did not restrict the meetings to broad strategy discussions, but got involved in a lot of day-to-day operational decisions for the various subsidiaries. One company manager commented:

> . . . [our company] has been run for many years on a highly paternalistic and centralized basis . . . all major decisions, including those that determine product lines overseas, are still made at the very top.
> To illustrate, all capital expenditures . . . exceeding $600 must be approved by the board of directors.

The impression of generally high headquarters direction in dominant-product firms was supported to some extent by the ratings of headquarters direction obtained from executives. Although the results are not statistically significant owing to the sample size, they are interesting in that none of the five dominant-product firms was low in headquarters direction, whereas six of the 21 multiple-product firms were (see Table 4).

The reason for the tendency toward great headquarters direction in dominant-product firms appears to be twofold. First, because of the crucial importance of a single product to the existence of the company, headquarters management of the dominant-product firm has a particular interest in closely watching all decisions that might influence sales and profits for this product. Second,

TABLE 4

Degree of Headquarters Direction by Degree
of Product Diversification

Headquarters Direction	Dominant-Product Firms		Multiple-Product Firms	
	Number	Percent	Number	Percent
High	3	60	9	42
Moderate	2	40	6	29
Low	0	0	6	29

in view of the narrow product line in dominant-product firms, headquarters of a dominant-product firm can more easily supervise
subsidiary activities than the management of a multiple-product
firm that markets a large variety of different products. A good
illustration is the difference between a firm selling essentially
one type of soft drink and a company selling a broad line of food
products. What makes centralized decision making easier in a
dominant-product firm is the fact that its management needs to
cope primarily only with geographical diversity, whereas a multiple-
product multinational firm must cope with two dimensions: geographical
diversity and product diversity.

Nature of the Firm's Products

The degree of headquarters direction varies by industry, as
was mentioned in the preceding chapter. More precisely, the nature
of a company's products seems to have an important bearing on the
extent to which a multinational enterprise centralizes its marketing
decision making at headquarters.
The sampled firms fall into two broad categories in terms of
the nature of their products: (1) food products and (2) nonfood
products, which include cosmetics, soaps-detergents-toiletries,
and soft drinks. Interviews with management revealed that strong
headquarters direction is more likely to occur in a firm in the nonfood
category than in a firm in the food category. Executives of nonfood
firms that were not already using strong headquarters direction
frequently mentioned a trend toward increased central control of

decision making. By contrast, several of the food firms in the sample which had previously used high headquarters direction were using moderate or low direction at the time of this study.

The quantitative data obtained provide some validation for the qualitative insight that nonfood product firms tend to have a higher degree of headquarters direction. Table 5 compares the ratings by executives of the degree of headquarters direction of marketing decision making in food and nonfood firms. About one-half of the nonfood firms were perceived to have high headquarters direction, compared to roughly one-third of the food companies.

TABLE 5

Degree of Headquarters Direction
by Nature of Products

Headquarters Direction	Food Product Firms		Nonfood Product Firms	
	Number	Percent	Number	Percent
High	4	36	8	53
Moderate	4	36	4	27
Low	3	27	3	20

The interviews with management revealed an explanation for the tendency toward comparatively stronger headquarters direction for the marketing of nonfood products: marketing programs for nonfood products seem to require less modification from country to country than do marketing programs for food products. Most executives of nonfood firms thought that target consumer groups, consumer attitudes, and product-use patterns differed very little from one country to another. The following quote illustrates this point and highlights the difference between nonfood products and food products:[5]

. . . . What can be done in detergents is not necessarily what can be done in margarine. In detergents, the public, regardless of country, class, colour or creed, would seem to have one dominant idea. They want their detergents to wash cleaner and that they often express as whiter. In margarine, a great deal depends on local taste and tradition.

In other words, food products are generally perceived to be more "culture-bound" than nonfood products. That is, they often become part of national culture, and their pattern of use and their meaning to consumers vary significantly from one country to another. As a result, local adaptation of marketing programs becomes necessary.

Of course, not all food products are equally culture-bound or require the same degree of modification in marketing program from country to country. Executives in the food industry were asked whether they could identify the types of products for which local custom tailoring of marketing programs was necessary. Listed below are the generalizations they developed:

1. The older the product category, the more likely that local taste differences will have developed over time.

2. If an industrial product replaces a product that was at one time homemade, then custom tailoring is likely to be necessary.

3. Products widely consumed at social gatherings are more likely to have developed distinctive local, cultural, and taste patterns.

4. If differences exist in the taste of raw materials from country to country, then these differences usually must be reflected in the taste of the resulting industrially prepared food product.

5. Products that are consumed mainly for their dietetic or medicinal properties require less local custom tailoring. Their consumption is influenced by the medical profession, which speaks an international professional language and which is more concerned with effectiveness than with taste. Even the final consumer is more tolerant in his taste requirements for such products as these.

6. Products that are bound to an industrial process are less likely to be custom-tailored. Evaporated milk, powdered milk, and frozen filet of sole are examples of products whose manufacturing process allows little room for taste variations.

On the basis of these generalizations and the comments of executives in other industries, any product might be classified at a specific point along a spectrum ranging from culture-free to highly culture-bound. Many nonfood products, such as detergents, soaps, and cosmetics, might be placed at the end of the spectrum called culture-free. Food products that are relatively young (such as pet food) or that did not replace homemade dishes when first introduced (such as powdered milk) might be classified as moderately culture-bound. Finally, highly culture-bound products would refer to those products whose consumers have developed distinctive preferences and traditions through long years of use. Coffee is a good example of a highly culture-bound product, as the following comments illustrate:

Coffee is an old product—350 years old in Europe—so local patterns and traditions surrounding coffee have

been built up over many years. As a result, local taste
preferences vary considerably from country to country,
and even within a country:
— the cafe au lait of France and Switzerland,
— the thin slightly acid taste of the Americans,
— the strong espresso in the small cup in Italy,
— coffee as a milk modifier in England and Australia,
— the smooth rich acidic taste of the Germans and the
Scandinavians.

Since highly culture-bound products, such as coffee, require
extensive custom tailoring of marketing programs to meet local
conditions, subsidiary management tends to play a dominant role
in determining the market program for such products. At least,
this situation appears to prevail in more mature multinational enterprises that have several decades of international experience. The
interviews with executives revealed that less experienced firms
encountered severe problems when they attempted to centralize
marketing decisions at headquarters for products that could be
categorized as highly culture-bound.

Although a multinational enterprise selling highly culture-bound
products tends to exert less direct influence on the marketing
activities of its subsidiaries, tight centralization of marketing
decision making for culture-bound products is not impossible per
se; it is just impractical. As Herbert Simon said, [6]

.... The two principal pulls in the ... direction
... of decentralization are, first, the fact that a
very large portion of the information that is relevant
to decisions originates at the operating level, and,
second, that the separation of decisions from action
increases the time and man-power costs of making and
transmitting decisions.

If, in fact, highly culture-bound products require marketing programs
that are heavily custom-tailored, a very extensive market intelligence system would have to provide headquarters personnel with
the detailed country-specific information that the job of custom
tailoring requires. Gathering marketing intelligence on this
scale would be costly and time-consuming at the least. Therefore,
firms selling highly culture-bound products tend to opt for greater
subsidiary autonomy and for reliance on integrative devices other
than headquarters direction.

New Products

Another product line factor that influences the degree of headquarters direction is whether a particular product is new to the firm

or already established in the market. Almost all the executives
interviewed mentioned, in one way or another, that their company's
basic policy regarding headquarters direction of marketing decisions
for new products was different from that for established products.
More specifically, in most firms, marketing decisions for new
products tended to be more strongly influenced by headquarters
than decisions for established products. The following comments
of headquarters executives reflect this attitude:

> We keep more control over a new product because we want
> to be sure before we put our name on anything.
>
>   *   *   *
>
> New products vs. existing products: this is a polarized
> thing as far as we are concerned at headquarters. We
> can leave our subsidiaries more on their own with existing
> products.
>
>   *   *   *
>
> We have centralized new product activities and decisions.
> The subsidiaries don't have the know-how and the budget
> for that. The philosophy behind this approach is to
> bring sophisticated marketing know-how to bear on the
> subsidiaries.

These comments allude to two major reasons for the greater
involvement of headquarters in the marketing of new products.
First, headquarters wants to protect the company name against
use on products that fail to meet certain standards. Second, the
development of new products and their introduction to the market
require skills that subsidiary management does not possess. In
other words, stronger headquarters direction is deemed to be
necessary to reduce the risk typically involved in introducing new
products.

At one extreme, all new product decisions are made by headquarters personnel with little subsidiary involvement. The following
comment is illustrative:

> The initiative for [new products] usually comes from
> headquarters. We will draw up the specifications,
> which—if necessary—may be modified by the subsidiaries.
> We have enough expertise at headquarters to know
> whether a product or a package will be accepted in a
> market. Occasionally, the initiative for a new product
> may come from the field, but all the development work
> would be done at headquarters.

One of the sampled companies has product managers at its European
headquarters who take responsibility for a group of products in all

the company's European subsidiaries. For new products, these regional product managers have a line position and make all decisions centrally, whereas for established products, they perform only an advisory and staff function. Consistent with the desire of headquarters to control all new product decisions is the regulation that subsidiary budgets not be negatively affected by new product activities; headquarters carries all the costs of developing new products and introducing them to the market, but the subsidiaries are given credit for sales of the new products. Once a new product has proved itself in the market, it becomes part of each subsidiary's regular product line, and the subsidiaries begin carrying the costs of production and marketing.

Even if headquarters executives do not take new product decisions completely out of the hands of subsidiary management, they are still deeply involved in each step of developing a new product and its marketing program. "New product decisions are the result of a very intensive dialogue between headquarters and subsidiaries," were the words used by one executive to describe the interactive process that takes place.

Although comparatively heavy headquarters involvement in marketing decisions for new products seems to be the general rule, there is an exception. It concerns the distinction between international products that are sold under the same brand name in a number of countries and purely local products that are developed for and marketed in only one country. In a firm that allowed its subsidiaries to carry purely local products, management indicated that headquarters did not interfere with the marketing decisions of its subsidiaries as long as the company name was not used on such products. The general trend among the industries studied seems, however, to be to reduce the number of purely local brands. The development at the subsidiary level of products that cannot be transferred to other countries is being discouraged, and attempts are being made to phase out local products and replace them with international brands.

The following comment of the European vice-president of one company reflects the general tendency toward greater multinational uniformity of products in the European area:

> We have widely differing product lines from country
> to country, due to leaving new product decisions com-
> pletely to the local managers in the past. A trend
> toward unification has now been initiated. In the
> development of new products, we consciously pursue
> a European or even worldwide strategy.

Consonant with this strategy, headquarters issued to its subsidiaries elaborate regulations for new product activities, from which the following guidelines have been excerpted:

All new product activity in [European] markets is subject
to approval by the [European regional headquarters]
and must be covered by the appropriate new product
proposal and approval as set out in these procedures
. . . .
    As a general rule, it will be our policy to coordi-
nate as far as possible the launch of [new] products
within all [European] markets, and the [regional head-
quarters] will establish . . . a timetable for approval
of local market introduction proposals . . . together
with a detailed timing schedule for all necessary
actions leading up to the launch date . . . .

MANAGEMENT STYLE

"Executives in charge of company destinies do not look exclusively at what a company might do and can do. . . . they sometimes
seem heavily influenced by what they personally want to do."[7] In
other words, the strategy of a multinational enterprise and the
organizational structure and process chosen to implement it cannot
be divorced from the personality, values, and aspirations of the
firm's top executives. That is, the relationship between headquarters
and the subsidiaries of a multinational enterprise can be expected to
be influenced by purely personal factors to a certain extent.
    Although no attempt was made to find quantitative evidence
for the impact of personal factors on the degree of headquarters
direction, the interviews and observations in the sample firms
conveyed the impression that the management style and the personality
of the senior executive in charge of international operations can be
powerful determinants of the roles played by headquarters and
subsidiary management in decision making. In several firms, the
attitude of a particular headquarters executive appeared to have
a dominant influence on the degree of headquarters direction. In
these firms, whether headquarters control was high or low seemed
to depend not on such factors as product diversification and product
nature, but on the personal inclinations, or management style, of
a single senior executive.
    The extent to which personal aspirations may influence the
degree of headquarters direction of decision making is illustrated
by the following comment of the President of the regional headquarters
of one of the sampled firms:

The role of . . . [headquarters] in the future will very
much depend on who is in charge of the office. My
predecessor saw the role of headquarters vis-a-vis
our local subsidiaries simply in terms of three C's:

> Coordination, Communication, and Counseling. When
> I took over here last year, I added a fourth big C:
> Control. I get more involved in the operations of our
> countries, and I could imagine that somebody following
> me might get even more involved.

Subsequent interviews with subsidiary executives of this firm
confirmed that headquarters direction had grown stronger since
this executive had arrived at headquarters. The General Manager
of one subsidiary said:

> Up to a year ago, there was no centralization. All
> decisions were locally made . . . . Today, our steps
> are prescribed by the central office. It's more than
> coordination; the central office has a tendency to
> unify local strategies . . . . We are centralizing.
> The number of people in the central office is growing;
> this means less autonomy for local management . . . .
> Centralization is going to continue and will be helped
> by our new information system.

This comment shows how the personal desire of the regional headquarters president to exercise control permeated the entire organization
and led, for example, to a larger headquarters staff and to a new
information system. Subsidiary managers reacted negatively to
this increase in headquarters direction, their objections being
mainly of two sorts. First, they resented their own personal
aspirations to freedom of action being endangered, and, second,
they felt that stronger headquarters direction would weaken the
organization's ability to respond to local market needs. A typical
comment was, "When you are in . . . [headquarters], everything
seems to be the same. When you are in the country itself, you
see tremendous differences."

These objections highlight a twofold problem that may arise
when the personal aspirations of the senior executive influence
the "modus operandi" of the organization. [8] First, a conflict may
exist between two sets of personal values: those of the headquarters
executive and those of the subsidiary managers. One set of values
cannot be satisfied indefinitely to the detriment of the other without
hurting the firm's overall effectiveness. Even if the desire of the
headquarters executive for control is consistent with the practica-
bility of strong central control—as determined by such impersonal
factors as the nature of the firm's products—tight headquarters
direction may be inopportune if it severely endangers the motivation
of subsidiary managers. Second, a conflict may exist between the
preferred management pattern of the senior executive—for example,

headquarters direction and program standardization—and the pattern that would be the most sensible economically—autonomy and program adaptation, for example. If this conflict is not dealt with, it will eventually hurt the market performance of the firm.

OUTSIDER INFLUENCE

Outsider influence may be a factor affecting the degree of headquarters direction in two situations. The first is when the multinational enterprise has less than full ownership of its foreign subsidiaries. The second is when the multinational enterprise forms its subsidiaries by acquiring already existing local firms.

The ability of headquarters to influence foreign operations may be severely limited if the multinational firm, rather than wholly owning its foreign subunits, has entered into a joint venture with local partners. "A local joint venture partner is rarely a completely passive shareholder."[9] A partner whose interests appear to be harmed by the policies of headquarters is likely to make himself heard, even if he holds only a minority interest.[10] In such a case, hierarchical authority is of little or no avail to headquarters; it must be replaced by efforts to persuade the outsider to go along with headquarters policies.

Stopford and Wells note that marketing-intensive multinational firms have a strong preference for wholly owned subsidiaries. One of the principal reasons that they discovered for this preference is precisely the lack of unambiguous headquarters control which is inherent in joint-venture agreements.[11] The data gathered in the present study confirm the preference for wholly owned subsidiaries. Of the 27 sampled companies, only three operated to any extent with subsidiaries that were not wholly owned; and even in those cases, the parent firms still held majority interests in the subsidiaries. Thus, the influence of outsiders resulting from limited ownership was not a significant concern among the companies studied here.

Another dimension of outsider influence was discovered, however, which seems to affect the degree of headquarters control over subsidiary operations. Those companies which had entered European markets predominantly or entirely through the acquisition of existing local firms tended to exercise less headquarters control over marketing decisions than firms that had established their own European subsidiaries. Headquarters executives in those companies described this effect as a severe handicap to integrating worldwide operations. Even in acquired subsidiaries that were wholly owned, outsider influence seemed to exist which worked as an obstacle to strong headquarters direction of decision making. Differences in product lines which existed both among the acquired subsidiaries and between

the subsidiaries and the parent company typically necessitated
allowing the subsidiaries considerable autonomy in marketing
decision making. Attempts to harmonize product lines over time
and to tie foreign operations together through systems transfer turned
out to be difficult.

The experience of a major U. S. food firm that attempted to
enter the European market through acquisition illustrates the sort
of problems encountered in managing acquired subsidiaries. In
its U. S. operations the company had developed fairly comprehen-
sive internal systems for marketing planning, budgeting, and control.
When it tried to use the same systems in its newly acquired European
subsidiaries, however, it encountered considerable resistance from
the managers of the acquired firms, who had been accustomed to
operating quite differently. Even as the years passed, the company
never quite succeeded in overcoming this resistance. Earlier
research indicates that this problem is quite common. Business
International Corporation noted in an early study on foreign acquisitions[12]

> The most serious problems [in managing acquisitions]
> usually arise when the new parent attempts to intro-
> duce new operating and control procedures that will
> unify the practices of the subsidiary and the parent.
> . . . the reasons given by the acquired firm for
> failure to comply are diverse and ingenious, ranging
> from the excuse that "it may work for you, but it's no
> good here, " or the obvious fact that it costs more
> money, to the plea that the new system will conflict
> with local company and tax laws.

In the food firm described above, the process of integrating
the foreign subsidiaries with the rest of the company was painfully
slow. Moreover, the company has not been able to rationalize
the disparate product lines being sold by its various subsidiaries
around Europe. Nor has it achieved an extensive transfer of product
concepts from the United States to the European scene. These
problems of harmonizing the marketing activities of acquired foreign
subsidiaries and the parent firm are not too different from the difficulties encountered with domestic acquisitions. As Mace and
Montgomery pointed out in their study, [13]

> Most of the administrative jobs of integration involved
> in acquisitions were described as difficult, but one
> area which seemed particularly perplexing was the
> integration of the marketing activities. Sales-oriented
> executives explained that this was due to the fact

that the problems involved the heart of any business,
namely, sales.

In view of these postacquisition problems, a multinational
enterprise that strives for unification of its foreign operations and
unquestioned headquarters influence on decisions would seem
well-advised to concentrate not only on having full ownership of
its subsidiaries but also on establishing its own subsidiaries rather
than acquiring existing local firms. If acquisitions are necessary
for growth, the primary assets that a multinational enterprise in the
consumer packaged goods field should probably look for in the firms
it acquires are a strong sales force and a well-established distribution network that can be used for marketing a similar line of products
in all countries of a geographical area, such as Europe. Paying a
lot of money for the good will associated with local brand franchises,
particular types of products, or well-established internal management systems is felt to be a questionable investment because of
the seeming difficulty of blending these intangible assets into the
business of the multinational enterprise.
Obtaining quantitative verification of the qualitative impression
that acquisitions tend to reduce the degree of headquarters direction
of marketing decisions proved difficult. Only three of the firms
studied had grown entirely through acquisitions; the rest had either
established subsidiaries themselves or used a mixture of acquiring
and establishing. Table 6 shows a cross-tabulation of executives'
ratings of headquarters direction and the origin of their firms' subsidiaries. It seems to support the qualitative statements above, in

TABLE 6

Degree of Headquarters Direction
by Origin of Subsidiaries

Headquarters Direction	Self-Established Subsidiaries		Both Self-Established and Acquired Subsidiaries		Acquired Subsidiaries	
	Number	Percent	Number	Percent	Number	Percent
High	7	70	4	31	1	33
Moderate	1	10	6	46	1	33
Low	2	20	3	23	1	33

that firms that did not rely on acquisitions for growth but established
their own subsidiaries were rated more often as having a high degree
of headquarters direction than firms that relied partly or exclusively
on acquisitions.

SUPPLY INTERDEPENDENCE

One strategy a multinational enterprise uses to gain a competitive advantage is to attempt to lower its manufacturing costs through
rationalization of production.[14] The enterprise may, for example,
concentrate the production of parts or of final products in a small
number of countries instead of letting each subsidiary produce all
products that it needs for its own market. Such a strategy of
rationalizing production entails supply interdependence among the
subsidiaries.

Executives of the sampled firms indicated in interviews that
the degree of supply interdependence among subsidiaries affected
the extent to which headquarters controlled marketing decision
making. In order to test this qualitative impression, the ratings
given by executives on the degree of headquarters direction were
compared with the degree of supply interdependence.* The results,
presented in Table 7, confirm that the degree of supply interdependence influences the degree of headquarters direction of marketing
decision making.

The interviews explained why high supply interdependence
coincided with high headquarters direction. In a firm that supplied
all its European subsidiaries from just two manufacturing plants,
executives related that headquarters involvement was necessary
primarily for two reasons. First, it prevented the manufacturing
subsidiaries from being burdened unreasonably with requests for
product modifications from other subsidiaries. Second, it prevented
the manufacturing subsidiaries from making unilateral product policy
decisions, an important constraint since the requirements of more

---

*Supply interdependence was measured by obtaining for each
European subsidiary of each firm (a) the percentage of production
output shipped to other European subsidiaries and (b) the percentage
of sales made with products supplied by other European subsidiaries.
The figures for all European subsidiaries of each company were
weighted by the subsidiaries' sales volumes and then combined
into an "average degree of supply interdependence." For the
sampled companies, this average ranged from zero to 65. The
categories "low," "moderate," and "high" designate averages of
zero through 10, over 10 through 40, and over 40, respectively.

TABLE 7

Degree of Headquarters Direction by Degree of
Supply Interdependence

| Headquarters Direction | Supply Interdependence | | | | | |
| | Low | | Moderate | | High | |
	Number	Percent	Number	Percent	Number	Percent
High	1	14	4	50	5	100
Moderate	4	57	1	13	0	0
Low	2	29	3	37	0	0

than one national market had to be met. Generally speaking then, if the product decisions of one subsidiary can influence greatly the activities and performance of other subsidiaries, joint decision making will be demanded by the subsidiaries that are affected, and headquarters is likely to be involved, if only as a clearing house of ideas. Apparently, such involvement of headquarters in product decisions then tends to spread to other elements of the marketing program.

Most executives interviewed emphasized that although supply interdependence leads to greater headquarters involvement in decision making, it does not make it impossible to manufacture different products for different country markets. The single fact that the subsidiaries do not all manufacture for themselves, however, creates an incentive for headquarters to influence product policy decisions in the direction of standardization.

ORGANIZATIONAL STRUCTURE

The formal organizational structure of any firm influences the relationships among its subunits. Thus, it was conjectured that the organizational structure of the multinational enterprise could be expected to influence the relationship between headquarters and the subsidiaries in marketing decision making.

Stopford and Wells have shown that the organizational structure of a multinational enterprise evolves in a distinctive sequence as direct investments abroad increase in importance.[15] They identify three stages: (1) the autonomous subsidiary stage, (2) the international division stage, and (3) the global organization stage.

At the autonomous subsidiary stage, which marks the beginning, direct investments are made abroad to penetrate or protect foreign markets that cannot be adequately served by exports. The executives who are sent out to manage these first subsidiaries typically enjoy virtually unlimited autonomy for decision making and action.[16] Among the factors that account for this high degree of autonomy, two are particularly important. First, since these initial investments abroad are typically small and not critical to the success of the company, headquarters management feels little need to introduce controls or to interfere in the subsidiary's operations. Second, headquarters would find it difficult to institute a control system at this stage because executives at headquarters are unlikely to have experience in managing foreign operations.

The second stage develops as the foreign subsidiaries grow in size and importance, and pressures to introduce controls emerge. Typically, the firm creates an international division at headquarters which is more or less equal in status to the other major divisions of the company.[17] The international division, which is essentially an "umbrella" for all of the company's foreign operations, is charged with the responsibility of coordinating and controlling the activities of the subsidiaries.[18] The creation of an international division is therefore a step toward organizational consolidation of the firm's international operations.

Generally, the international division is a transitional structure.[19] As long as it exists, the multinational enterprise actually operates as two separate companies—one with a domestic orientation and one with a foreign orientation. This split between domestic and foreign operations tends to interfere with overall strategy planning and communications within the enterprise as the international division grows in size and as product and area diversity abroad increases.[20] Often, the multinational enterprise responds by dissolving the international division. This move is the beginning of the global organization stage, in which the multinational enterprise attempts to bridge the gap between domestic and foreign interests and to plan its strategy on a consistent worldwide basis.

Four major types of global structure may emerge when the international division is dissolved. If product diversity is relatively low, but area, or geographical, diversity and sales volume abroad are significant, geographical or area divisions may develop as the company's primary organizational element. If, however, high product diversity abroad is coupled with significant international volume, worldwide product divisions may evolve. Still other companies have chosen a mixture of area and product divisions in designing their global structure. More recently, a few multinational enterprises have experimented with a fourth type of global organization called a "grid" structure. It is characterized by the use of multiple reporting relationships to accommodate conflicting demands for product, area, and functional coordination.[21]

All of the multinational enterprises that were investigated in this study have reached either the international division or the global organization stage. The question therefore becomes: How does the degree of headquarters direction of marketing differ among (1) companies that have an international division to which all its foreign subsidiaries report directly, (2) companies that have a product organization with product divisions responsible worldwide for a specific product or product group, and (3) companies that have an area organization with regional offices responsible for the subsidiaries in a particular geographical area? These regional offices could be either geographic subdivisions of an international division or parts of a global structure. They are lumped together in the same category because their management of foreign subsidiaries is typically very similar. A global structure with area divisions often evolves from an international division with geographic subdivisions. Stopford and Wells mentioned that this evolution "consists primarily of adding an extra level of senior general managers." The regional subdivisions of the international division are transformed into area divisions. "The control procedures developed in the international division are often transferred to the central office by merging the staff groups in the international and central offices.[22]

Interviews with company executives did not provide evidence that organizational structure is related to the degree of headquarters direction (see Table 8). In fact, executives in different companies made contrasting statements about the effect of organizational structure on headquarters involvement in decision making:

> The move to product divisions meant some more centralization . . . . This gives us greater professionalism at headquarters. We now have a professional manager in . . . [corporate headquarters location] who cares only for one single product group in all countries . . . . All major marketing decisions are made by the product manager; the general manager in each country will be responsible for implementation and administration.
>
> *   *   *
>
> We have discussed worldwide product divisions. That raises the question – Can you dictate a campaign for a product for the whole world? Most of the decisions now, with an area structure, can be made instantaneously because we are close to the field. One man in . . . [corporate headquarters] could not make his presence felt.

Apparently, high headquarters direction can be achieved with any one of the basic organizational structures. The major explanation for this phenomenon seems to be that the categories of international organizational structure–international division, product organization,

TABLE 8

Degree of Headquarters Direction by Type of
Organizational Structure

Headquarters Direction	International Division		Product Organization		Area Organization	
	Number	Percent	Number	Percent	Number	Percent
High	2	67	2	50	8	42
Moderate	0	0	2	50	6	32
Low	1	33	0	0	5	26

and area organization—are so broad. Each encompasses a number
of different organizational arrangements that can influence the
process of decision making and the degree of headquarters direction
in a variety of ways.

For example, an international division to which subsidiaries
report directly—without an area or a product subdivision as inter-
mediary—can be a very effective mechanism for tight headquarters
control, but only if the number of subsidiaries reporting is small.
As the number and size of reporting subsidiaries grow, the span of
control of executives in the international division broadens, and
effective headquarters direction becomes more and more difficult.
One executive in an international division said, "It's tough to
manage the growing business. We are about five years late in
going to a regional structure. We will, in the future, move to a
regional structure."

For a firm at the verge of making such a major structural change,
central control by the international division is a less manageable
job than for a company in the early phase of the international
division stage. Hence, the fact that a multinational enterprise
manages its foreign subsidiaries through an international division
cannot be taken, per se, as an indication of either high or low
headquarters direction. The same is true for multinational enterprises that have chosen global structures with area or product
organizations. Both area and product organizations comprise
various organizational arrangements. For example, area divisions
may include product subdivisions with regional product managers
or product coordinators at headquarters. The existence of such
subdivisions enhances the possibilities for central control.

One generalization about the relationship between headquarters
direction and formal organizational structure can safely be made,

however. Unless the number of foreign subsidiaries and the volume of the company's international business are both small, the desire of headquarters to control marketing decision making tightly will complicate the organizational structure. A look at a highly centralized multiple-product company, whose organization chart is presented in simplified form in Chart 2, will demonstrate this point.

The company uses geographical areas, product groups, and functions to structure its headquarters organization. Reporting to the marketing manager of each product division are product coordinators and subsidiary coordinators. Each product coordinator is responsible for all activities concerning the marketing of one product in all the subsidiaries reporting to his product division. Each subsidiary coordinator, by contrast, has the function of coordinating the marketing activities for all products in one subsidiary. The reporting relationship between the subsidiaries and the product divisions is determined by the relative importance of the various product groups to the subsidiaries' business. Each subsidiary reports to the product division responsible for the product group that contributes the most to that subsidiary's total sales volume.

Assume, for example, that Subsidiary 1 in Chart 2 makes 60 percent of its total sales in products of Product Division I. It will then report to Product Division I, which takes line authority over Subsidiary 1 and is also responsible for implementing policy guidelines issued by the functional departments of Area A (for example, Finance), which are not specialized by product. Product Division II and the other Product Divisions maintain line authority over Subsidiary 1 as far as decisions affecting their products are concerned. Reporting to the Marketing Manager of Product Division I is Subsidiary Coordinator 1. In spite of this reporting relationship, his responsibilities are not defined in product terms; rather, he performs administrative and coordinating functions for all aspects of Subsidiary 1 business.

Such a complex structure clearly contains a number of potential sources of conflict. Apparently more serious, however, than inter-departmental conflicts at headquarters (among product divisions, for example) are delays in headquarters-subsidiary communications. Subsidiary managers considered the process of decision making to be slow, overly bureaucratic, and over-centralized. They were adamant in their criticism, as the following statement of one manager shows:

> The Subsidiary Coordinator comes much too often and
> the Marketing Manager too infrequently; we would
> like more direct contact with him . . . . Also, we
> would like more contact with the Product Coordinators.
> We don't know what's going on for a product in another

CHART 2

Headquarters Organization in a Multiple-Product Firm

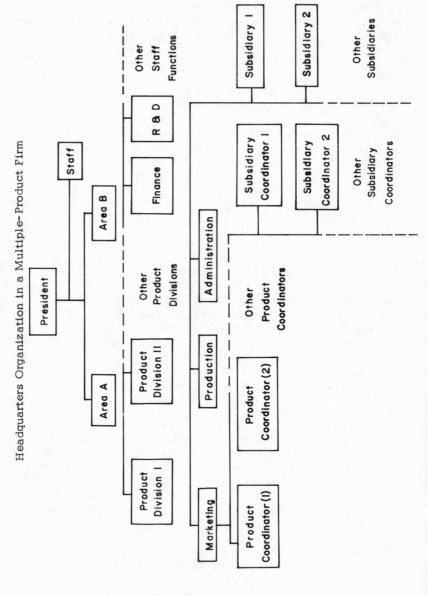

country. Once we were having serious problems with
. . . [Brand X]. We were still searching for the most
appropriate advertising approach here, while in France,
where they had a similar problem, they were already
shooting the TV spots. The Subsidiary Coordinator
doesn't know about these things, but the Product
Coordinators and the Marketing Manager do . . . .
   We would rather deal directly with the Marketing
Manager, and we finally have to in order to get a
decision. Many times we waste a whole day in meetings
at headquarters with Subsidiary Coordinators and Product
Coordinators without getting anywhere and then five
minutes past 5 PM somebody from the higher level sticks
his head into the room and settles the whole thing
within five minutes. There are too many levels involved,
too many people; this often leads to delays in decision
making . . . . We are managed through pretty close
supervision by headquarters. Headquarters desire
to interfere at times extends to ridiculously trivial
things. We argue a lot about details, but we hear
little about the strategy . . . . There should be more
freedom of action for the subsidiaries and agreed-upon
strategic guidelines.

Headquarters management was well aware of these frictions. It
realized that the current organization and the extent of headquarters
involvement in decision making could be potentially damaging to
local motivation and initiative. No immediate change in organizational
structure or in the pattern of headquarters direction was envisioned,
though. Centralized decision making for the purpose of global
planning was regarded as more important than decentralization for
the sake of enhancing local motivation.

RELATIVE IMPORTANCE OF FOREIGN OPERATIONS

   For headquarters control over subsidiary activities to increase
as the importance of a firm's foreign operations grows would not
be an unreasonable expectation. In testing this reasoning, the
percentage of total sales coming from nondomestic markets was
chosen as a measure of the relative importance of foreign operations
to the firm. Alternative measures, such as the percentage of total
profits or the percentage of total net worth accounted for by the
foreign subsidiaries, proved to be less easily ascertainable and,
also, less reliable owing to the differences in accounting and
financing policies from one company to another.

TABLE 9

Degree of Headquarters Direction by Percentage of Sales
from Foreign Operations

Headquarters Direction	Sales from Foreign Operations (Percent)							
	0-15		Over 15-30		Over 30-45		Over 45	
	Number	Percent	Number	Percent	Number	Percent	Number	Percent
High	4	57	3	50	2	50	3	43
Moderate	2	29	1	17	0	0	3	43
Low	1	14	2	33	2	50	1	14

The company interviews did not show that the percentage of
foreign sales affected the degree of headquarters direction in one
way or the other. In particular, the interviews did not validate
the expectation that increasing foreign sales volume would lead to
stronger headquarters direction. In fact, the company with the
highest percentage of foreign sales placed particular emphasis on
decentralized decision making and developing strong country managers.
At one time, this firm had moved toward greater headquarters direction
in an effort to standardize advertising campaigns, but that policy
was relaxed when subsidiary managers reacted negatively. The
following comments were made at the firm's headquarters:

> Much of [our] success over the years can be traced to
> our policy of having strong country managers on the
> scene to run the marketing side of things in each market.
> We call this the concept of "the one-man show" . . . .
> When we realized that a trend toward standardization
> might jeopardize our ability to develop strong and
> effective general managers at the local level, we
> decided to back off a bit.

Table 9 shows a cross-tabulation of the executives' ratings
for the degree of headquarters direction and the percentage of sales
coming from foreign operations. The results of this quantitative
analysis are inconclusive. One explanation for the results may
be that all the sampled companies, though differing widely in
percentage of foreign sales, were already in advanced stages of
their multinational development; that is, they were beyond the
autonomous subsidiary stage. All of them, therefore, had already
recognized the need for some headquarters control of foreign
activities. The results might have been different had the sample
also included a number of less mature internationally active companies.

NOTES

1. For earlier research on such factors, see Richard John Aylmer,
Marketing Decisions in the Multinational Firm (doctoral dissertation,
Harvard University, Graduate School of Business Administration,
1968); John M. Stopford and Louis T. Wells, Jr., Managing the
Multinational Enterprise (New York: Basic Books, Inc., 1972).

2. Leonard Wrigley, Divisional Autonomy and Diversification
(doctoral dissertation, Harvard University, Graduate School of
Business Administration, 1970).

3. Ibid., p. III-7.

4. See ibid., p. III-9.

5. Comments of the Chairmen of Unilever Limited and Unilever N. V. in Unilever Limited, Style in Management: The Unilever Experience (London: Unilever Limited, Information Division, 1970), p. 4.

6. Herbert A. Simon, Administrative Behavior, 2d ed. (New York: The Free Press, 1965), p. 157.

7. See Kenneth R. Andrews, The Concept of Corporate Strategy (Homewood, Ill.: Dow Jones-Irwin, Inc., 1971), p. 104.

8. See ibid., p. 106.

9. Stopford and Wells, Jr., op. cit., p. 107.

10. See ibid., p. 107.

11. See ibid., pp. 107-13.

12. Business International, Acquisitions Abroad (New York: Business International Corporation, 1963), p. 26.

13. Myles L. Mace and George G. Montgomery, Jr., Management Problems of Corporate Acquisitions (Boston: Harvard University, Graduate School of Business Administration, Division of Research, 1962), p. 255.

14. See Stopford and Wells, Jr., op. cit., pp. 58-62.

15. See ibid., Ch. 2.

16. Ibid., p. 20.

17. Raymond Vernon, Sovereignty at Bay: The Multinational Spread of U. S. Enterprises (New York: Basic Books, Inc., 1971), pp. 125-26.

18. Stopford and Wells, Jr., op. cit., p. 21.

19. Ibid., p. 25.

20. Ibid., pp. 24-25.

21. For more detailed treatment of these structures, see ibid., Chs. 3-6.

22. Ibid., p. 52.

CHAPTER

4

OTHER INTEGRATIVE
DEVICES

Theoretically, headquarters direction is sufficient to influence the behavior of subsidiary managers and to integrate the geographically dispersed operations of a multinational enterprise. The comments of managers of the sampled firms show, however, that to rely exclusively on headquarters direction is often impractical. Though headquarters direction is theoretically sufficient, it is not always necessary because other integrative devices are available to influence the activities of foreign subsidiaries. The sections that follow describe the use of corporate acculturation, systems transfer, and personnel transfer as integrative devices.

CORPORATE ACCULTURATION

Interviews with managers revealed that firms with a low degree of headquarters direction of marketing decisions often placed particular emphasis on establishing attitudes and behavior patterns in their subsidiary managers which would lead these men to make decisions that conformed to headquarters intentions. The following comments illustrate what happened in these enterprises:

> We don't need orders and policy manuals to tell our people out there what to do. They know it; not because we tell them but because they thoroughly understand and have learned to appreciate our way of doing business through long years of their association with this company.
>
> *   *   *
>
> This is a company of management by conviction; I don't remember ever telling somebody. I think it is a fair statement to say that this is one of the most centralized

operations not because we have people breathing down
each other's necks but because we have set up a system
and structure of checks and balances and we put our
managers through an acculturation process.

In other words, these firms rely on subsidiary managers who are
thoroughly committed to corporate objectives and philosophy. They
have been "acculturated" to the company's business approach to an
extent that they can be allowed to run the firm's foreign subsidiaries
with relatively little overt direction from headquarters.

Among the companies studied, those with long years of multinational experience and heavy dependence on foreign sales and
profits were often particularly adamant about the value of corporate
acculturation as an integrative device. For example, the following
comments were made in the firm with the longest multinational
experience and the heaviest dependence on foreign operations of
all the enterprises studied:

Our managers are scattered throughout the world. They
are of every conceivable nationality; they speak many
different native tongues; and they represent a hodge-
podge of cultural backgrounds. In order to avoid chaos
and be successful on a worldwide basis, the multinational company must somehow find a way to develop
in its managers a strong sense of corporate identification
and spirit that transcends all of this diversity . . . .
It's necessary to develop a sense of personal loyalty to
the company and commitment to its corporate goals.
    In a multinational company, . . . personal links
and loyalty of the top people in the subsidiary companies
are of particular importance. Head office cannot hold
a world together and exercise control only by the formal
infrastructure and the official instruments of control.
There have been times in the past, and they may come
again, when the whole cohesion in a multinational
company such as ours depended more on personal loyalty
than on anything else. This personal relationship and
loyalty must be cultivated through intensive personal
contacts . . . . Sometimes it is essential for top management to give in to an argument in order not to endanger
such loyalty.
    Loyalty and personal links are more easily built up
in companies where people are not only motivated by
profit or by satisfaction in their individual job, but by
a common motive that is called in German the "Geist"
of a company or what the French call "esprit de corps"

. . . . A company which has it—and I obviously assume
it is positive and inspiring—has a definite advantage over
those who do not. This is particularly true in a multinational company where you have to give the man in the
far away periphery a particular motive to give more of
himself than he would normally give in the interest of
something as distant as a company several thousand
miles away.

These comments highlight how corporate acculturation functions
as an alternative or a supplement to headquarters direction of
decision making. In the absence of corporate acculturation, a
firm would have to increase headquarters control in order to maintain
unity of its multinational business operations. [1] The comments also
suggest that the extent to which worldwide operations can be integrated efficiently through the exercise of headquarters authority
alone has practical limits. Simon expressed the same idea:
"Administrators have increasingly recognized . . . that authority,
unless buttressed by other forms of influence, is relatively impotent
to control decisions in any but a negative way . . . the task of
supervision becomes hopelessly burdensome. "[2] Thus all multinational enterprises must rely on some combination of integrative
devices, rather than on any one device exclusively. Moreover,
if headquarters direction and corporate acculturation are used
together, management must recognize that they are not only supple-
ments but also, to some extent, antagonists. An overuse or abuse
of headquarters direction may hurt corporate acculturation; headquarters direction may at times have to be curtailed to maintain the
motivation and the organizational loyalty of subsidiary managers.
Interviews with company executives revealed that corporate
acculturation of subsidiary managers is largely the result of long
training periods and promotion through various levels within the
company. In the firm that provided the comments above, a man
might typically have spent 10 to 15 years—first as a salesman, then
as an assistant product manager, a product manager, a group product
manager, and a marketing manager—before finally being assigned
to the position of subsidiary general manager. He will also have
had at least one assignment, of two or three years in length, with
the marketing group at corporate headquarters. Top management
emphasized the importance of this particular stage in the man's
career.

It is important, and it should be a basic part of any
management development plan, that those people who
are destined to occupy key positions of responsibility
in a subsidiary company should spend part of their

career at head office in order to be injected with the
particular "bug" of that company. That is why in a
multinational company the hiring of top people from
another company is delicate.

In addition, the company would send the man to numerous programs
offered within the company for management development. After this
process of training, headquarters can be sure that he understands
and accepts "the company's way of doing business."

Accomplishing such corporate acculturation takes time,
skill, and deliberate effort. The first step is to ensure
that all managers, regardless of background or nationality,
can speak a common "company language" of professionalism.
Our internal systems for market planning and budgeting
play a key role in teaching such a common language.

Corporate acculturation can also be enhanced by frequently
transferring company personnel across borders, either for long-term
assignments in other countries or for short-term visits among headquarters and subsidiary personnel. Kuin confirms the role of such
transfers in his report on multinational management practices at
Unilever N. V.: "International transfers in the first five or ten
years of managers' careers are part of this process . . . [of corporate
acculturation]."[3]

The transfer of uniform systems for planning, budgeting, and
reporting to the subsidiaries and the transfer of personnel not only
enhance corporate acculturation, they also can facilitate headquarters direction of decision making. Moreover, systems transfer
and personnel transfer are in and of themselves important sources
of international competitive strength.

SYSTEMS TRANSFER

Terminology

Before the marketing planning and control systems observed in
the sampled companies can be discussed in any detail, a few terms
must be clarified. In the literature, a distinction is often drawn
between planning (deciding what to do) and control (assuring the
desired goals are achieved).[4] As Anthony points out, however,
this distinction is not very useful because planning and control
activities occur together in practice. He says that "although
planning and control are definable abstractions and are easily
understood as calling for different types of mental activity, they

do not relate to separable major categories of activities actually carried on in an organization, either at different times, or by different people or for different situations."[5]

In his framework for analyzing planning and control systems, Anthony distinguishes among "strategic planning," "management control," and "operational control."[6] Strategic planning is described as a nonroutine, staff-oriented, top-management activity concerned with the overall objectives and direction of the company. Management control concerns the task of obtaining and using resources for specific programs of action within the guidelines established by strategic planning.[7] It includes such activities as formulating budgets, planning staff levels, formulating advertising programs, and planning product modifications; it can generally be described as the planning and control process associated with the ongoing administration of the company. Operational control focuses on specific tasks or transactions, such as scheduling and controlling individual jobs through a shop; it is a routine activity involving primarily the supervisory level.

The investigation here of the planning and control process of multinational enterprises assumed that, by definition, strategic planning was primarily a headquarters responsibility and that operational control was predominantly a subsidiary activity. Since most of the interaction between headquarters executives and subsidiary executives involved in the planning and control process occurs in the area of management control, the investigation focused on activities that fall into that category.

The Importance of Planning and Control Systems

In roughly two-thirds of the investigated firms, the executives interviewed attached high importance to the use of marketing planning and control systems as an integrative device and as a tool for gaining competitive strength. The following comments are illustrative:

> Everyone must understand and use the annual planning format, which is our Bible. It's the cornerstone of our activity. This has helped me educate our men and make them fit for competition more than anything else. This format I want them to understand, to use, to take to bed with them, and to brand on their pyjamas.
>
> *   *   *
>
> There is a lot of learning that occurs as a result of the give and take that takes place among our local, regional, and headquarters marketing personnel in

the process of hammering out our marketing plans and
budgets. The planning, budgeting, and control systems
provide a disciplined framework or process for analyzing
marketing situations and problems. In this process our
regional marketing people function a bit like honeybees
carrying the pollen of ideas and judgment from one market
to another. And by the time local, regional, and headquarters management all reach agreement on a marketing
plan and budget for the coming year, we are fairly certain
that the plan is a pretty sound one.

The enthusiastic comments about the importance of marketing
planning and control systems are not surprising. These systems
create a way of looking at and analyzing problems; they impose an
internal discipline that may be called "marketing orientation,"
"good management," or "profit consciousness."
Particularly in the more mature multinational enterprises with
long years of international experience, executives at headquarters
stressed the educational value of well-developed marketing planning
and control systems, besides their function of keeping headquarters
management abreast of subsidiary developments and assuring integration and global planning. This aspect of marketing planning and
control systems was mentioned, for example, by all four food firms
that could qualify as mature multinational enterprises. The executives felt that these systems enabled subsidiary management to
anticipate problems better, to recognize opportunities and threats
in the environment, to plan for appropriate action, and to improve
subsidiary performance generally. Again and again, executives
in the mature multinational enterprises said that the factor that
really set their firms apart from local competitors was a better and
more disciplined system for planning and implementing local marketing
efforts. Their management control systems, they felt, provided a
"common language" that everybody in the geographically dispersed
subunits of the enterprise could understand and use in analyzing
business problems. Moreover, these systems were designed to
accomplish several purposes simultaneously:

1. To achieve thorough analysis of local marketing and
competitive conditions as a basis for the design of local marketing
programs;
2. To achieve systematic and comparable market analysis in
each country so that significant differences in local market conditions could be identified before marketing approaches borrowed
from other countries were tried;
3. To enhance the corporate acculturation of local, regional,
and headquarters executives with diverse backgrounds and nationalities, and to facilitate the international transfer of marketing skills
and attitudes;

4. To make sure that top management's overall corporate
marketing objectives could be achieved without headquarters'
needing to issue extensive command-type directives to local
subsidiaries.

Thus the marketing planning and control systems used by the mature
multinational enterprises, together with long years of on-the-job
training and experience, helped to ensure that local managers would
become inner-directed and make marketing decisions that would be
appropriate both to local market needs and to the company's long-term
international objectives.

The Scope of Planning and Control Systems

All of the companies whose executives were interviewed used
some form of formal planning and control system to coordinate their
foreign marketing operations. Furthermore, most executives felt
that the procedures and formats of management control used by all
subsidiaries had to be uniform in order to assure comparability of
marketing plans and to facilitate the preparation of consolidated
reports at headquarters. For the same reason, practically all of
the companies required their subsidiaries to follow the same accounting principles and to submit reports in the same language, usually
the language of the country where the parent company was located.
In most firms, the primary constituent of systems for management control of marketing activities is the annual marketing plan
and budget. The purpose and the scope of the annual planning and
budgeting process vary considerably, however, from one firm to
another. About a dozen firms had either very rudimentary systems
or very elaborate systems. For the firms with very rudimentary
management control systems, the major purpose of the annual
marketing plan and budget seemed to be to forecast year-end results
on the basis of past performance and environmental developments
rather than to formulate programs for future action. Budgeting and
planning were largely the responsibility of staff personnel or the
finance and control departments in these firms. The plans and
budgets were mainly quantitative in nature, emphasis being given
to financial figure work, particularly in such areas as capital
expenditures and cash flow. Explanatory comments, if present at
all, often simply rephrased the quantitative data.
In contrast, the purpose of the marketing planning and budgeting
process in firms with very elaborate systems was to establish specific
objectives and programs of action, to which subsidiary managers
would be committed and against which their performance would be
evaluated. As a natural consequence, line management in marketing
was heavily involved in the planning and budgeting process. Although

the annual budget contained figure work that was very detailed and
included profitability analysis by product or product group, it also
contained an essential qualitative element. In addition to explaining
the figure work, the text discussed and justified actions planned
for the coming year, identified critical success factors, spelled out
responsibilities and deadlines for implementation of the plan, and
established yardsticks for measuring performance.

A look at the procedures followed in one of the companies will
show just how elaborate the planning and budgeting process can be:
Planning and budgeting activities followed a set of instructions
communicated to the subsidiaries in a loose-leaf volume called the
"Marketing Budget Manual, " more familiarly known within the firm
as the "marketing bible. " The first step in the annual budgeting
process was for each subsidiary to prepare a general fact book for
its country and a product fact book for each major product that it
sold. The general fact book provided a uniform format for gathering
information on market factors that could be expected to affect the
overall marketing activities of the subsidiary, such as population
composition and trends, economic climate, industry outlook, competition, and marketing legislation. Each product fact book contained
product-specific information on such factors as total market size,
market segments, market shares and trends, consumption habits,
consumer attitudes, pricing, and distribution channels.

Starting with the fact books, the subsidiary managers were
expected to propose both long-term and next-year marketing budgets,
which were to follow an internationally standardized format. The
long-term budget contained the broad outlines for marketing objectives and strategies, together with a forecast of sales, expenses,
and profits, for the next six years. The preparation of the budget
for the coming year was described by one headquarters executive
as the "real meat" of the whole planning operation. He went on to
say:

> The annual marketing plan is a very elaborate document
> . . . . It is prepared and discussed in two stages, first
> as a skeleton budget and subsequently as a final budget.
>   The skeleton budget is prepared and discussed in
> early summer and was introduced to avoid the company
> being forced, under pressure of time, into accepting
> basic policies solely because it would be too late to
> change when the final marketing budget is presented
> in the autumn. The purpose of the skeleton budget is
> to make sure that market and head office see eye to eye
> on the basic strategy before detailed work begins. The
> final budget contains specific plans, figures, and
> details. These budgets are discussed with regional

management and the various functional departments at
head office . . . . The discussion of such budgets
may go to considerable detail; for example, . . . we
might examine at the final budget discussion all TV
scripts, media schedules, and research techniques.
But part of the discussion is for advice and only part
for final approval by regional management. Where
the dividing line goes is rather difficult to say; this
often remains a secret shared by nobody.

Once approved, the budgets form the program
for the coming year. Their execution is the responsibility of the market head. The market could now be
left alone. However, in the competitive world of
today, . . . there is constant need for change . . . .
It is generally accepted that major changes will be
discussed with head office.

The actual formats used in annual planning and budgeting
exercises are highly confidential documents and therefore can not
be presented here in detail. Chart 3, however, which is an abbrevi-
ated and disguised check list from a company manual, gives an idea
of the major points covered in an annual marketing plan.

In the industries studied, marketing planning and budgeting
systems tended to become more elaborate as the relative importance
of international operations to the company as a whole increased.
This trend was emphasized by many of the executives interviewed.
Moreover, a number of the companies in the sample were either
just in the process of shifting to a more detailed system of international management control or had recently made this shift. Also,
this trend was confirmed by the more mature multinational companies
in the sample—those with several decades of multinational experience
and with sales and profits resulting predominantly from foreign
operations—they had the most highly developed marketing planning
and budgeting systems of all the firms in the sample. The most
elaborate marketing planning and budgeting system was found in a
firm that had established its first foreign subsidiary more than a
hundred years ago and derived roughly 97 percent of its total sales
and profits from foreign operations.

Preparation of Annual Marketing Plans and Budgets

The preparation of marketing plans and budgets follows a specific
pattern in most multinational enterprises. Planning and budgeting
generally start in the subsidiaries and work upward from the lower
organizational levels to regional and corporate headquarters. Most

CHART 3

Checklist of Important Factors in the
Annual Marketing Plan

PROBLEMS/OPPORTUNITIES: What are the key problems and opportunities?

Product Mix	Sales Offtake
Pricing	Competitive Moves
Distribution	Market Development

OBJECTIVES: What do we want to achieve?

Product	Consumer Awareness
Sales	Offtake
Distribution	Positioning

MARKETING PROGRAM: What is the plan of action?

Product	Direct Marketing Mix
Pricing	Advertising Strategies
Sales Drives	

PRODUCT INFORMATION

Total Market	Sales Volume
	Unit Price
	Net Sales
Market Share ____ %	Gross Profit
	Direct Selling
	Direct Marketing
Distribution ____ %	Deals
	Product Contribution

Source: Adapted from a planning manual of a multinational enterprise.

of the executives interviewed at headquarters and in the subsidiaries favored this approach. They felt that initiation of planning at the operating level was imperative; it ensured the commitment of subsidiary managers to the goals and measures specified in the plans. Furthermore, planning from the bottom up was deemed necessary in order to build local market conditions into the budget.

Almost all companies go through roughly similar steps in preparing their marketing plans and budgets. Subsidiary management draws up a budget for the coming year and marketing plans for the next two to five years, in most cases according to a uniform format provided by headquarters. Plans and budgets are then submitted to headquarters for approval, and the subsidiary general manager, his marketing manager, and often his financial manager typically make a visit to headquarters at this time. After being approved, plans and budgets become (1) yardsticks for evaluating subsidiary performance and (2) the framework within which subsidiary managers can make decisions.

The preparation of marketing plans and budgets, like most major decisions in any organization, is not the task of a single individual. Rather, these plans and budgets evolve through the interaction of many individuals in different departments and at different organizational levels. [8] All of the executives interviewed stressed the point that the planning and budgeting process involves a lot of interaction between subsidiary and headquarters personnel. Headquarters management usually has a fairly good idea about the general contents of the subsidiaries' marketing plans and budgets before their official presentation. In most companies, headquarters personnel visit the subsidiaries during the preparation period to discuss budgeting procedures, to assist in the preparation, and to ensure that plans and budgets not only meet local market requirements but also take global company interests into account. The executives acknowledged that visits and discussions during the preparation period fulfilled an important function in that they welded together the subunits of the multinational enterprise. In fact, if there was one point on which the participating executives agreed almost universally, it was that the give-and-take built into the annual planning and budgeting cycle was at the very heart of multinational marketing.

Even though the prevailing "from the bottom up" approach leaves much of the initiative for planning and budgeting to subsidiary management, headquarters executives influence in many ways what enters the plans. Their insistence on uniform formats for marketing plans and budgets is just one of these ways; personal visits during which headquarters personnel informally communicate headquarters expectations to subsidiary management are another, and the predetermination of profit targets is still another way. Most of the companies interviewed issued certain guidelines for marketing planning and budgeting to their subsidiaries at the beginning of each budget cycle. The executives were questioned about the type of guidelines issued and the extent of their use. As Table 10 shows, more than one-half of the firms studied establish limits for the planning of capital expenditures, and more than two-thirds issue targets for profit margins to their subsidiaries, prior to budget

TABLE 10

Guidelines Issued for Marketing Planning and Budgeting
Prior to Budget Preparation

Guideline Areas	None		Occasional		Detailed	
	Number	Percent	Number	Percent	Number	Percent
Capital expenditures	7	35	2	10	11	55
Profit margins	3	15	3	15	14	70
Advertising and promotion expenditures	9	45	3	15	8	40
Prices	11	55	3	15	6	30
Personnel expenditures	10	50	4	20	6	30
Total annual marketing plan	6	30	3	15	11	55

preparation. Less frequently used are guidelines for the budgeting
of advertising and promotion expenditures, prices, and personnel
expenditures.

Communications Between Headquarters
and Subsidiaries

The quality of a firm's management control system depends
largely on the effectiveness with which company objectives, guidelines, expectations, decisions, and results are communicated
throughout the organization. [9] In a multinational enterprise, with
its wide geographical dispersion of operating units, maintaining
an effective flow of communications between the subsidiaries and
headquarters becomes a demanding and critically important task.
The quality of the communications system determines the ability
of headquarters to control and to integrate subsidiary activities,
to formulate and implement global strategies, and to utilize the
experience accumulated in conducting business in many different
markets.

Information and instructions are exchanged between headquarters
and the subsidiaries in a number of forms, ranging from formal
written reports, to less formal personal interviews, and finally to
the grapevine. [10] Each form of communication is necessary and
suitable for a specific purpose, though headquarters and subsidiary
managers feel that the forms differ in importance. When the executives interviewed were asked to rank various forms of communication
according to their importance, more than three-quarters–both at
headquarters and in the subsidiaries–mentioned personal contact
as the most important (see Table 11). Telephone calls, telex, and
letters were ranked second in importance by more than half of the
managers interviewed, whereas formal reports were usually rated
as the least important. Formal reports, they felt, often reflected
only what had previously been agreed upon in personal interviews
among headquarters and subsidiary personnel.

Though regarded as the least important form of communication
by the majority of the managers interviewed, formal reports are
the part of the communications system on which subsidiary and
headquarters executives alike typically spend the greatest amount
of time and effort. Most headquarters ask their subsidiaries for
a great quantity of written information: almost all the companies in
the sample required regular information from their subsidiaries
about new product activities and production methods, and roughly
half of the firms regularly collected information about advertising
techniques and promotion approaches, distribution methods, and
market data (see Table 12).

TABLE 11

Importance of Various Forms of Communication

Forms of Communi- cation	Most Important		Moderately Important		Least Important	
	Number	Percent	Number	Percent	Number	Percent
Personal contact	17	77	5	23	0	0
Telephone, telex, and letters	3	13	13	59	6	28
Formal reports	2	9	3	13	17	78

The annual marketing plan and budget is just one way of collecting all this information. In addition to these annual reports, most multinational enterprises require their subsidiaries to submit to headquarters a number of other regular reports, such as quarterly and monthly budgets, a monthly general manager's report on all aspects of subsidiary operations, and monthly or even weekly sales reports. A variety of special one-time reports may also be required: reports on significant competitive developments in the local markets, on personnel changes, or on change of suppliers, for example.

Headquarters managers feel that all this information must be collected in order for them to be able to perform cross-border comparisons and to establish a basis for multinational planning. Moreover, as was true of annual marketing plans and budgets, frequent reporting is seen by many headquarters executives as a means of educating subsidiary managers to watch closely the development of their operations. What is regarded as necessary and important information at headquarters may, however, be perceived as irrelevant and burdensome to collect at the subsidiary level. [11] A number of subsidiaries complained that the information demands of headquarters were excessive:

Headquarters has a tendency to ask for ridiculously detailed information . . . . With all the data we are sending up they must get lost in details.

*   *   *

We are wasting our time on an infinite number of specialized reports for the central office.

*   *   *

Too many picayune problems have to be submitted to
headquarters and are resolved in the weekly top management conferences. Headquarters gets involved in too
many day-to-day operational decisions for the various
subsidiaries.

The burden of work which reporting to headquarters imposes on
subsidiary management is not all that is at the heart of these and
other critical comments. Many subsidiary managers resent detailed
reporting because they interpret any headquarters request for elaborate
information as an attempt to limit subsidiary autonomy. As interviews
at headquarters revealed, this interpretation was in many cases a
valid one. Companies that were moving toward greater headquarters
direction typically initiated this move with requests for more frequent
and more detailed reports from their subsidiaries.

Besides complaining about too much reporting to headquarters,
subsidiary managers frequently expressed concern over receiving
too little information from headquarters. Many subsidiary executives
felt that the flow of communications between headquarters and the
subsidiary was out of balance—more specifically, that headquarters
did not provide sufficient information on the marketing experience
gathered in other countries.

TABLE 12

Frequency and Type of Written Reports Sent
to Headquarters

Type of Information	No Reports		Occasional Reports		Regular Reports	
	Number	Percent	Number	Percent	Number	Percent
New products	3	14	0	0	18	86
Production methods	2	10	1	5	18	86
Advertising and promotion	7	33	2	10	12	57
Distribution	8	38	4	19	9	43
Market data	7	33	2	10	12	57

> The opportunities to see how the company is doing it
> in another country would be an invaluable help in terms
> of giving one new ideas and making one familiar with
> a wide variety of possibilities . . . . We don't get
> any such information on a regular basis, not even on
> request. I have made several pleas to headquarters
> about this, but no reaction.

*   *   *

> The dissemination of marketing experiences . . .
> in other countries has been developing slowly only
> over the past two or three years. It is still not
> regular, though it should be, and still an exception
> rather than a rule.

Few of the companies investigated seem to have given much thought, top management attention, or financial support to the development of a systematic approach to collecting, evaluating, and disseminating the multitude of experiences gathered in their various subsidiaries. As a result, attempts to communicate such experiences and the extent to which and the manner in which experiences should be shared were not defined. Executives at a number of company headquarters admitted that so far they had been concerned more with the collection of data on their subsidiaries than with the feedback of information to the subsidiaries.

Practically all headquarters and subsidiary executives did, however, emphasize that the broader experience base and the opportunity for making wiser decisions that resulted from knowledge of success and failure in a large number of markets were among the major competitive advantages of being multinational. Thus, finding more effective ways of disseminating to subsidiaries the market experience gathered in various countries would appear to be an important task for headquarters in the future.

PERSONNEL TRANSFER

The transfer of marketing personnel from headquarters to subsidiaries and from one subsidiary to another is a way of conveying marketing skills across borders and of integrating dispersed foreign operations. Executives in more than two-thirds of the firms studied felt, however, that personnel transfer played a minor role, in comparison to systems transfer, in their firms' efforts to gain competitive strength as a multinational enterprise.

Long-term and short-term transfers of personnel seem to differ in importance. Company interviews suggest that long-term assignments of executives abroad are being deemphasized; more especially,

there is a marked deemphasis on assigning home country nationals
of the parent firm to key positions in foreign subsidiaries. [12] The
opinion of many executives was that the long-term assignment of
marketing personnel abroad is too costly, often produces conflict,
and is generally not very effective as a means of transferring skills.
These executives mentioned, however, that top management's
attitude toward the long-term transfer of personnel had changed
over time. In fact, they conveyed the impression that the personnel
policies of multinational enterprises often develop through the
following three rough phases:

1. When the company first goes abroad, the tendency seems
to be to prefer home country nationals for key positions in subsidiaries. "Those are the men we can trust and understand," is a
statement that describes this tendency.

2. Later, there frequently is a radical shift in policy, reflected
by such statements as "We want to employ local managers in the
subsidiaries to the maximum extent possible." Long-term transfers
of personnel, particularly home country nationals, is discouraged;
at the same time, systems transfer becomes more important as a
means of maintaining control over subsidiary operations and of
ensuring integration of the firm's worldwide activities.

3. The more mature multinational enterprises with long years
of international experience seem to take a very pragmatic view,
which results in a mixture of nationalities both at headquarters
and in the subsidiaries. [13] In these companies, the question,
"What is your policy with regard to transferring people in general
and with regard to the nationality of subsidiary managers in particular?" is typically answered with a comment like the following:
"We don't have any rigid policy. We don't care what passport a
man carries as long as he is a company man." More important than
anything else for the transfer of marketing skills and the integration
of the business in these companies is the internal acculturation of
their managers through a combination of long training periods and
a heavy stress on well-defined planning and control systems.

In contrast to their skeptical view of long-term transfers of
personnel, most executives felt that short-term international expo-
sure was an important means of facilitating the transfer of marketing
skills. Many firms concentrated on providing opportunities for
subsidiary managers to visit other markets and for headquarters
executives and subsidiary managers to visit each other.

In almost all the companies studied, frequent visiting took
place between headquarters and the subsidiaries. Generally,
however, headquarters personnel visited the subsidiaries more often
than subsidiary managers visited headquarters. Although the overt
purposes of the visits were to amplify and clarify reports written by
subsidiary personnel and to solve specific problems in subsidiary

operations, they also contributed to overall cooperation and coordination simply because they enabled headquarters and subsidiary
personnel to get to know each other better.

Personnel encounters among subsidiary managers from different
countries are increasingly recognized as means of solving some of
the problems of disseminating information on experiences in other
markets. To this end, a number of companies have instituted annual
or biannual meetings of general managers and marketing managers
of all subsidiaries during which each subsidiary presents the
highlights of its marketing plan for the coming year. These meetings
allow an intensive interchange of information; moreover, they enhance
each manager's sense of belonging to a worldwide organization.

Typically, visits and meetings last only a few days. In many
companies they are supplemented by classroom seminars for subsidiary managers and/or on-the-job training lasting several weeks.
These management development activities serve a multiple purpose:
they educate and acculturate subsidiary managers, and they facilitate
"horizontal" communication—communication among managers from
different parts of the multinational enterprise who are at the same
hierarchical level and have the same functional responsibility. All
of the subsidiary executives interviewed commented enthusiastically
on these training activities. They felt that these activities allowed
them to broaden their horizons beyond their own local markets and
to develop a better appreciation of headquarters objectives and
actions.

INTERRELATIONSHIP OF INTEGRATIVE DEVICES

Short-term transfers of personnel occur for the most part in
conjunction with the annual planning and budgeting process. Thus,
the transfer of management control systems leads to increased
personnel transfer; by the same token, personnel transfer influences
the effectiveness of systems transfer.

This relationship between personnel transfer and systems
transfer is just one variation on a general theme that has emerged
during this study: there is a great deal of interaction among the
various integrative devices. A number of the findings discussed
earlier in this chapter are corroborative. Corporate acculturation,
for example, determines how much headquarters direction is necessary; and the overuse of headquarters direction may hinder corporate
acculturation. Effective planning and control systems and the
transfer of headquarters personnel to the subsidiaries can facilitate
headquarters direction. Systems transfer and personnel transfer,
in turn, are closely interrelated and, together, determine the
degree of corporate acculturation.

In view of this interaction among the integrative devices in multinational marketing, the question for management is not which device, but rather which combination or "mix" of devices, to use to integrate worldwide marketing activities. Although one ingredient in this mix, such as headquarters direction, may be dominant, the critical management task is to include the other ingredients in their proper proportions. The task is to find an internally consistent integrative mix in which headquarters direction, systems transfer, personnel transfer, and corporate acculturation are combined in such a way that they mutually support their individual integrative effects.

NOTES

1. See Pieter Kuin, "The Magic of Multinational Management," Harvard Business Review, November-December 1972, pp. 89-97.

2. Herbert A. Simon, Administrative Behavior, 2d ed. (New York: The Free Press, 1965), p. 227.

3. Kuin, op. cit., p. 96.

4. See Robert N. Anthony, Planning and Control Systems: A Framework for Analysis (Boston: Harvard University, Graduate School of Business Administration, Division of Research, 1965), p. 10.

5. Ibid., pp. 10-11.

6. Ibid., pp. 15-21.

7. See ibid., pp. 15-19, 27-68.

8. See Simon, op. cit., pp. 221-22.

9. See Anthony, op. cit., p. 50.

10. See Michael Z. Brooke and H. Lee Remmers, The Strategy of Multinational Enterprise (New York: American Elsevier Publishing Company, Inc., 1970), p. 47.

11. See ibid., p. 53.

12. The same view is expressed by Kuin, op. cit., p. 90: "The time when practically all senior managers of an international company were citizens of the home country is past."

13. Ibid., p. 90.

5

STANDARDIZATION
OF MARKETING

The use of the integrative devices discussed in the preceding chapters will lead to different forms of integration. These forms represent varying degrees of uniformity and cohesiveness in the foreign operations of the multinational enterprise. In the marketing area, an important form of integration is the use by each subsidiary of the same marketing program for a particular product. Such standardization does not occur automatically, of course. Rather, it is the result of a conscious decision at headquarters and of deliberately employing the various integrative devices.

The extent to which marketing programs are standardized reflects the emphasis that firms give to headquarters direction in their "mix" of integrative devices. Corporate acculturation, systems transfer, and personnel transfer may quite possibly facilitate the implementation of a decision at headquarters to standardize marketing programs, because they will develop in subsidiary managers a better understanding of headquarters' intentions and a common business philosophy. Invariably, however, the standardization of marketing programs will be coupled with headquarters direction of decision making. This combination of standardization with headquarters direction was mentioned by the executives interviewed:

> The creation of multinational brands necessitates that many things are centrally decided at headquarters.
>
>   *   *   *
>
> We control our subsidiaries pretty tightly in order to achieve uniformity of image for our products around the world.

The standardization of marketing programs has been a controversial form of integration for a number of years. Both businessmen and academicians have debated whether such standardization is

advisable or feasible. While some observers emphasize the benefits
of standardized marketing approaches, [1] others point to the differences
in country conditions which may act as obstacles to such standardization. [2] In view of this debate, an attempt has been made to gather
empirical evidence of the extent to which standardization of marketing
programs actually takes place and also to investigate how external
market conditions affect the headquarters decision to standardize
or not standardize marketing programs from country to country.

EXTENT OF STANDARDIZATION

In order to measure the extent to which multinational enterprises
standardize their marketing programs internationally, executives
of the 27 companies sampled were asked to look at two countries
at a time and to judge how similar or different each element of the
firm's marketing program for a particular product was in those two
countries. A typical question was "How similar or different is the
packaging of Product X in the United Kingdom to its packaging in
Germany? – in Sweden? – in France?" The judgments of the executives
on this and other aspects of the firm's marketing program were obtained
as ratings on seven-point semantic differential scales, and the
consistency of their ratings was checked by interviewing more than
one executive in each company.

In analyzing the ratings obtained, each paired-country comparison, rather than each company, was treated as a single statistical
observation. With 27 companies and up to ten country pairs per
company, more than 200 observations were obtained for individual
elements of the marketing program. The ratings for all country pairs,
products, and companies were combined to create an index of international standardization of marketing decisions (see Chart 4). It
gives the percentage of all paired-country comparisons falling into
one of three categories—high standardization (ratings one, two, and
three), moderate standardization (rating four), or low standardization
(ratings five, six, and seven).

For the marketing program as a whole—that is, all program
elements viewed together—63 percent of the ratings fell into the
high standardization category and 27 percent into the low standardization category. Considerable variation in the extent of multinational
standardization existed, however, among the various elements of
the marketing program.

The standardization of product policy decisions—brand names,
physical characteristics of products, and packaging—appears to be
extremely high. The ratings for these marketing program elements
were confirmed in interviews with executives. They often indicated
that brands and packages in particular are usually highly standardized,

CHART 4

Index of Standardization of Marketing Decisions

Marketing Program Elements — Percent of Paired-Country Comparisons

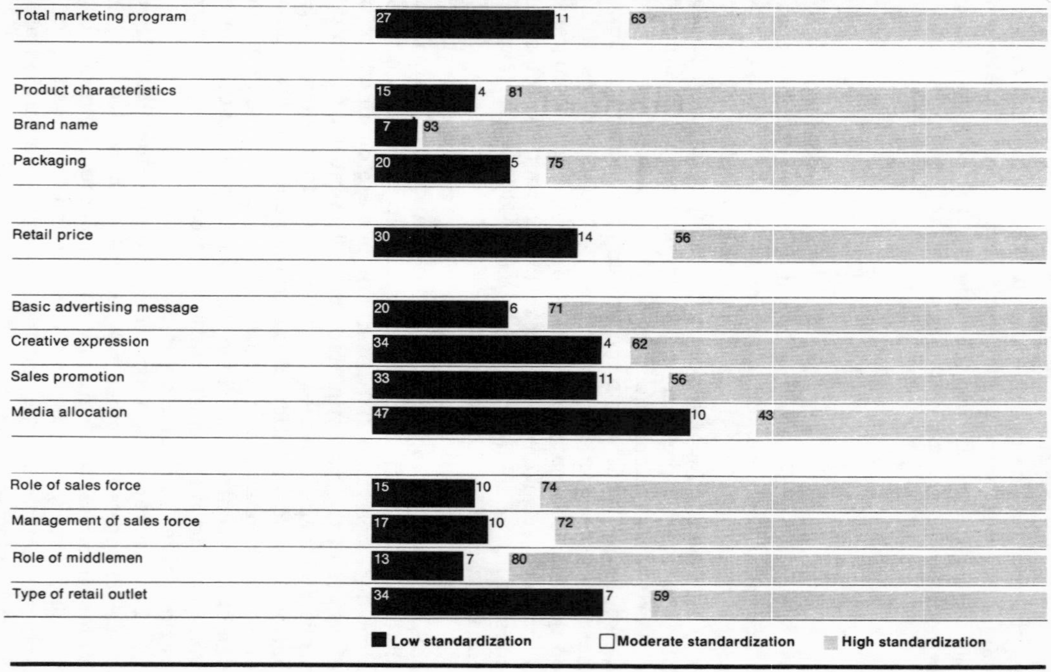

Marketing Program Elements	Low standardization	Moderate standardization	High standardization
Total marketing program	27	11	63
Product characteristics	15	4	81
Brand name	7		93
Packaging	20	5	75
Retail price	30	14	56
Basic advertising message	20	6	71
Creative expression	34	4	62
Sales promotion	33	11	56
Media allocation	47	10	43
Role of sales force	15	10	74
Management of sales force	17	10	72
Role of middlemen	13	7	80
Type of retail outlet	34	7	59

■ Low standardization   □ Moderate standardization   ▨ High standardization

both because of trademark considerations and because of the apparent
dream of most managements to some day have recognizable worldwide
brand franchises.

> With respect to branding, labeling, and packaging, . . .
> we have followed from the beginning a policy of strict
> uniformity . . . . We have never fallen deeply into the
> trap of having different brands in different markets for
> the same product or, what is worse, having the same
> brand for different products.
>   The same policy applies for labeling and packaging
> . . . .
>   The advantages are fairly obvious: by having uni-
> form brands and labels, we get much better international
> legal and trademark protection . . . . Lastly, there are
> the intangible advantages. On a regional basis, for
> example, in an area such as continental Europe, where
> there is an increasing degree of mobility on the part
> of consumers, . . . we find that brand and packaging
> uniformity can reinforce consumer recognition on a
> European-wide basis.
>   *   *   *
> Our policy for . . . new products will be to reproduce
> and launch these products in European markets as far
> as possible in the identical form and packaging . . . ,
> using the same marketing concept and approach.

In contrast to product policy decisions, pricing decisions tend
to be much more dissimilar from country to country. The following
comment of one executive is representative of a widely held view:

> Price is probably the marketing mix element which is
> most difficult to standardize because of country to country
> differences in freight, duty, taxes, trade practices,
> and competition. Unfortunately, in many instances,
> we have almost no discretion over what we charge in
> a particular market.

The standardization indices for advertising and promotion
decisions ranged from very high to extremely low. Almost three-
fourths of the executives felt that the basic advertising message
was highly standardized. A frequent practice among the sampled
companies was to require all subsidiaries to adopt the basic
advertising theme developed at headquarters, but allow them to
adapt the creative expression of that theme to their local market
conditions.

The least frequently standardized of all marketing decisions are those for media allocation in advertising budgets. One explanation is that the availability of advertising media still varies considerably among European countries. Commercial television time, for example, though readily available in Great Britain, is severely restricted in Germany and simply unavailable in Sweden.

Most ratings concerning channels of distribution fell into the high standardization category. Apparently, however, the similarity of distribution decisions from one country to another has been more accidental than intentional. One executive said "The distribution channels and the sales methods we use are quite similar in all European countries. But this is not because we make any special effort to have similarity, but simply because in all these countries there is only one sensible way in which our products can be distributed."

When executives were asked to rate the marketing program as a whole, the extent of standardization seemed to vary considerably by type of product. Cosmetics were the most highly standardized: 95 percent of the 41 ratings obtained from cosmetics firms indicated high standardization. In contrast, considerable local custom tailoring seemed to occur for certain food products. For example, 51 percent of the 37 ratings by executives in firms selling instant coffee showed low standardization.

MARKET CONDITIONS AND STANDARDIZATION

In view of the differing extent to which the companies standardized all of parts of their marketing programs, an obvious question is: What conditions might lead headquarters to aspire to either high or low standardization? Initially, the hypothesis that standardization would be higher the more market conditions were similar from country to country seemed reasonable. To test this idea, an attempt was made to assess, for each product, how similar or different the following market conditions were from one country to another:
- Target consumers for the product.
- Use pattern for the product among consumers.
- Stage of the product in its life cycle.
- Retail structure.
- Availability of advertising media.
- Marketing legislation.

To measure the similarity of market conditions, executives in the sampled companies were asked to look at two countries at a time and judge how similar or different they thought market conditions were for a certain product. Again, their judgments were obtained as ratings on a seven-point semantic differential scale ranging from

"quite similar" (rating one) to "quite different" (rating seven).   In
a number of companies, more than one executive was asked to give
ratings, and the responses were highly consistent within each
company.   When the same type of product was examined in more
than one company, market condition ratings were compared across
companies.   The result, again, was a high degree of congruence.

In analyzing the data obtained, the ratings on the seven-point
scale were compressed into three categories: high, moderate, and
low similarity.   When the ratings on the degree of cross-border
similarity of market conditions were compared with the ratings for
standardization of the total marketing program (see Chart 5), two
relationships emerged.   First, a high degree of cross-border similarity
of market conditions seemed to occur together with high standardization of marketing programs.   This relationship was the strongest for
such products as cosmetics, soft drinks, and detergents.   Second,
the tendency to custom-tailor marketing programs when market
conditions were dissimilar was not as marked as the tendency to
standardize when conditions were similar.   More specifically, a
number of companies seem to be engaging in cross-border standardization despite strong differences in market conditions.   This
approach was the most pronounced for certain food products, such
as soups, cheeses, and desserts.

When executives were questioned further about how various
local market conditions affected the degree to which they modified
their marketing programs, a number of them suggested that the
first modifications made are usually those about which management
has no choice.   There are many examples of such obligatory custom
tailoring of marketing programs.   Legislation in some countries
prohibits consumer deals, retail price maintenance, and certain
distribution methods for a product.   In other countries, particular
advertising media and retail outlets do not exist.   Any of these
factors may require a company to change its marketing approach
from country to country.

Such obligatory custom tailoring should be distinguished from
discretionary custom tailoring, in which management is not compelled
to make changes but chooses to make them in response to subtle
differences in local market conditions.   For example, products are
sometimes repositioned or their prices changed according to where
they are in their life cycles or what market share they hold in various
countries.

In the opinion of many executives interviewed, discretionary
custom tailoring is less common than obligatory custom tailoring.
In fact, as Chart 5 suggests, many marketing programs are standardized
in spite of significant differences in market conditions.   A widespread
rule seems to be: When in doubt standardize; modify only those parts
of the marketing program which must be changed because the barriers
to standardization are insurmountable.

CHART 5

Similarity of Market Conditions Compared with Standardization of Total Marketing Program

Market condition	Number of paired country observations	Degree of similarity of market conditions	Percent of standardization of the total marketing program (rounded off)		
			Low	Moderate	High
Target consumers	147	High	16	6	78
	57	Low	51	19	30
Use pattern	129	High	9	8	83
	63	Low	51	15	34
Stage in product's life cycle	141	High	18	10	71
	59	Low	30	5	65
Retail structure	68	High	26	6	68
	72	Low	31	18	51
Media availability	96	High	19	12	69
	75	Low	30	5	65
Marketing legislation	38	High	13	13	74
	28	Low	54		46

■ Low   ☐ Moderate   ▨ High

84

Frequently personal opinions about standardization rather than systematic analysis of market similarities and dissimilarities seemed to determine whether marketing programs were standardized or custom-tailored. One executive said

> You seem to be looking outside the company for explana-
> tions as to why we use such a standardized marketing
> approach. What you should be doing is to look inside
> the company. I grant you that our subsidiary people
> spend a lot of time studying their respective markets
> and thinking about their competitors, and I suppose
> these things should theoretically have a greater bearing
> on what we do. But in my view, the real reason why
> we currently use such a standardized approach is because
> [the president of the firm's European operations] makes
> all the key marketing decisions, and he just wants it
> that way because he's a great believer in international
> standardization.

This attitude has led to a number of spectacular market failures. For example, three well-known U. S. food companies, which sell soups, cereals, and cake mixes, went through remarkably similar experiences when they first tried to break into European markets. Initially, all three established beachheads in England, which seemed the easiest place to start because of similarities in language and customs. From England, they intended to expand onto the Continent. They entered England with products and marketing programs very similar to those which had been successful in the United States. The process of marketing decision making was highly centralized; key decisions were usually made at headquarters in the United States. All three companies found the going very rough mainly because their approach of high standardization and high headquarters direction did not take account of fundamental differences between the two countries' markets.

Subsequent attempts of these firms to enter continental markets met with equal difficulty. While it reassessed the situation, each company decided to cut down its European efforts in the mid-1960s. More recently, each of these firms has once again stepped up its operations in Europe, this time using more custom tailoring of marketing programs and less direction of local marketing activities from headquarters.

While reducing the extent of headquarters direction, management has given much greater attention to designing an effective uniform system for planning and controlling marketing decisions which each subsidiary must use in developing its marketing program. In other words, systems transfer seems to have taken the place of head-quarters direction as the major integrative device. Moreover, the standardization of marketing programs per se has been deemphasized in favor of standardizing the process through which these programs are developed.

The standardization of the process of marketing decision making through systems transfer is an important alternative and a complementary form of integration to the standardization of marketing programs. One headquarters executive elaborated on this idea as follows:

> A total standardization of all the elements of the marketing mix is hardly thinkable. On the other hand, the intellectual method used for approaching a marketing problem, for analyzing that problem, and for synthesizing information in order to arrive at a decision can absolutely be standardized on an international basis.
>
> It is desirable that marketing decisions be as decentralized as possible toward the field of economic battle. Nevertheless, if decision making is done in each country according to the same intellectual process, it can be more easily understood by headquarters management: a standard process eliminating guesses and the subjective side of marketing permits one to arrive more easily at the standardization of certain elements of the marketing mix.

Some companies will, however, be fortunate enough to be able to identify and operate in product categories whose marketing requirements are highly similar from country to country. In particular, companies whose products are culture-free will probably be successful in employing a standardized marketing program. Knowing whether to standardize or to custom-tailor, however, requires some mechanism for systematic cross-border analysis of market conditions. Thus international marketers should give high priority to developing and refining such a mechanism; trial and error is a costly alternative. Systematic cross-border analysis would probably add more discretionary custom-tailoring of local marketing programs to the obligatory custom tailoring that already occurs in response to local laws and other barriers to standardization.

REASONS FOR STANDARDIZATION

Since standardizing marketing programs is risky when market conditions are dissimilar and since systematic cross-border analysis would undoubtedly be costly, the question arises whether the standardization of marketing programs is really worth trying. The

arguments in favor of program standardization fall into two major
categories: (1) better marketing performance and (2) lower marketing
costs. 3

The first argument in favor of standardization is that a marketing
strategy that has been successful in one country can, if transferred
to another country with similar market and competitive conditions,
lead to better consumer and trade acceptance, a larger market
share, and higher profits in the second country. One executive
said, "You try to get maximum mileage out of a successful campaign."
Or, in the words of another manager, "We want to avoid a duplication
of effort. What we are trying to do in standardizing our approach is
stop reinventing the wheel."

In addition, standardization helps to establish a uniform worldwide image for a company's products. Such uniformity seems to be
a major concern of many firms in the consumer packaged goods
industries. In Europe, overlap among countries in terms of products,
consumers, trade customers, and advertising media is increasing;
it will therefore facilitate and may even necessitate standardization
of marketing programs. As the headquarters marketing director of
one company said at a conference held for the company's advertising
managers

> . . . [A] point which favors an international approach
> is the overflow of products from one country to another.
> This overflow has been greatly facilitated by the setting
> up of the European Common Market. Whereas in the past
> we tried to keep the product of one market in that market,
> today it has become virtually impossible.
>
> The EEC has also facilitated the overflow of people
> from one market to another. The tourist movement is
> ever growing in momentum . . . . These people are more
> and more likely to see the same or similar products in
> different markets.
>
> The increasing overflow of advertising media also
> suggests increasing possibilities for international adver-
> tising campaigns. For example, 45 percent of all Dutch
> TV sets and 85 percent of all TV sets in German-speaking
> Switzerland are regularly tuned to TV programs from
> Germany. Or, consider that Paris Match has a regular
> circulation in Belgium and Switzerland.
>
> The growth of international companies and the
> policies that some have of using international approaches
> tend more and more to make consumers aware of inter-
> nationalism, to accept it, and even to keep alert for
> standardized marketing approaches.
>
> The advent of international groupings in the trade
> such as voluntary chains and multiples may bring about

increased pressure from their side for international
approaches on the part of manufacturers.

The second argument in favor of the standardization of multinational marketing is that it may lead to savings on product design,
on packaging, on premiums for sales promotion, and in advertising
production costs, especially for TV commercials. Moreover, in
the short run, a less elaborate local staff may be required to adminis-
ter a standardized plan than to formulate a custom-tailored plan.

Many of the executives interviewed, however, were doubtful
about the potential for such savings in the consumer packaged
goods industries. In fact, in only one of the companies were
executives able to offer evidence of specific savings that had
resulted from the standardization of marketing programs. In many
companies, executives pointed out, advertising production costs
for consumer products are relatively low compared with the costs
of buying advertising space or time. The potential savings on
product design are considered to be more substantial, but still not
as great in the consumer packaged goods industries as in the
consumer durable goods or the industrial goods industries. And,
unlike many companies in the latter industries, consumer packaged
goods companies usually cannot attain significant manufacturing
scale economies through standardized products.

NOTES

1. See, for example, Norman Heller, "How Pepsi-Cola Does
It in 110 Countries," in John S. Wright and Jac L. Goldstucker, eds.,
New Ideas for Successful Marketing (Chicago: American Marketing
Association, 1966), pp. 694-700.

2. See, for example, Robert D. Buzzell, "Can You Standardize
Multinational Marketing?" Harvard Business Review, November-
December 1968, pp. 102-13.

3. See ibid., p. 105.

6

SUMMARY AND CONCLUSIONS

Research began with the proposition that in order for a multi-national enterprise to be successful, it had to (1) integrate its geographically dispersed operations and (2) transfer critical skills to its subsidiaries (marketing skills, in this case). Four major integrative devices were identified: Headquarters direction of decision making, corporate acculturation, systems transfer, and personnel transfer. It was concluded that these integrative devices and the process of integration are in and of themselves important means of transferring marketing skills across borders.

The study focused on two controversial variables in multi-national marketing: (1) headquarters direction of marketing decision making and (2) standardization of marketing programs, which is a form of integration. The aim was to find empirical evidence for the degree to which marketing-intensive firms employ headquarters direction of marketing decisions, to determine what factors influence whether decisions are made at headquarters or at the subsidiary level, and to discuss the use of the other integrative devices. In addition, an attempt was made to assess the extent to which multi-national enterprises use standardized marketing approaches and how market conditions affect headquarters' decision to standardize or custom-tailor marketing programs from country to country. The investigation centered on the European operations of 27 multinational enterprises in the food, soft drink, soap-detergent-toiletry, and cosmetics industries.

The study revealed a high degree of headquarters direction for marketing decisions. Moreover, the prevailing opinion of the executives interviewed was that headquarters direction would increase rather than decrease in the future. This tendency toward headquarters direction may result in part from a natural desire for power at regional and corporate headquarters and in part from an understandable urge to keep close watch over those elements of

the business which are the most critical. In the industries investigated, marketing decisions are clearly critical.

The tendency toward headquarters direction was found to be
related to several corporate factors: the product line of the firm,
the presence of outsider influence, and the degree of supply interdependence among subsidiaries. In addition, although no quantitative
evidence was collected, the management style of senior executives
in charge of international operations seemed to influence the degree
of headquarters direction.

The study also revealed a generally high degree of standardization of marketing programs. Moreover, it was apparent that the
standardization of marketing programs typically goes together with
headquarters direction of marketing decisions, and that use of the
other integrative devices may enhance such standardization. In
comparing the extent of standardization of marketing programs with
the degree of cross-border similarity of market conditions, two
conclusions emerged. First, high cross-border similarity of market
conditions seemed to occur together with high standardization of
marketing programs. Second, custom tailoring of marketing programs
when market conditions were dissimilar was not as marked as the
tendency to standardize when conditions were similar.

Many of the companies in the sample seemed to be basically
centripetal in approach. At one time or another, they tried to
centralize substantial parts of the decision-making process at
headquarters. At the same time, they also tended to standardize
all or part of their marketing programs for particular products. A
major reason for this approach is the need to create a uniform product
image in a geographical area that is characterized by an increasing
tendency for consumers, trade customers, and advertising media to
overlap from one country to another.

Discussions with executives brought to light some further
reasons for high standardization and high headquarters direction.
To the marketing executive at regional or corporate headquarters,
centralizing decision making at headquarters and using hierarchical
authority to achieve standardized marketing programs may appear
to be a much more expedient way to transfer know-how and to
integrate foreign operations than trying to coordinate a variety of
different viewpoints and a variety of custom-tailored marketing
approaches. Moreover, there is the attractive but seldom verified
argument that insistence on standardization can lead to significant
cost savings in such areas as the production of advertising materials,
product design, and sales promotion. Finally, there is the idea
that "if it works successfully in country A, there is no reason why
it shouldn't also work in country B." Thus many headquarters
executives have a tendency to minimize local market differences
and say "Let's standardize."

Many firms seem to engage only in obligatory custom tailoring, that is, they modify only those parts of the marketing program which must be modified because of patently obvious barriers to standardization, such as unavailability of advertising media or prohibitive legislation in a certain country. Discretionary custom tailoring in response to more subtle differences from country to country, such as dissimilarities in the stage of a product's life cycle, is less common.

At this point, an attempt will be made to draw some tentative conclusions about the use of integrative devices and the standardization of marketing programs. These conclusions are based more on personal observations and impressions than on quantitative data collected.

The multinational enterprises examined in this study can be classified into two broad categories: (1) firms selling products that are highly culture-bound and (2) firms selling products that are only moderately culture-bound or culture-free.* Food products seem to be more culture-bound that nonfood products. Within the food category, old products, products that were previously made at home (such as soups), appear to be more culture-bound than young products, products that did not replace a homemade product when first introduced (such as powdered milk). The two types of multinational enterprise differ in the way in which they manage the marketing function.

Firms whose products are culture-free or only moderately culture-bound, such as the four cosmetics and the three soft drink firms studied, tend to use a combination of high headquarters direction and high standardization of marketing programs. In the opinion of the executives of these firms, this approach is the most logical and the most efficient because differences in the relevant market conditions from country to country are considered to be small. Evidence of the appropriateness of high headquarters direction and high standardization is provided by the one cosmetics firm and the one soft drink firm studied which are not yet using this marketing approach. They are currently making strong efforts to increase headquarters direction and standardization of marketing programs, because they are not satisfied with the results of their current practice.

Firms with products that are culture-free or only moderately culture-bound and with long years of practicing high headquarters direction and high standardization occasionally seem to have encountered difficulties when they tried to extend their product

----

*The definition of what, precisely, constitutes a product that is culture-bound or culture-free is in itself an issue for research.

lines into categories that required more custom tailoring. The difficulties arose because headquarters domination of marketing decisions had to be replaced by greater reliance on the judgment of subsidiary managers. Headquarters management had to learn to depend more heavily on integrative devices other than headquarters direction and to develop headquarters-subsidiary relations that were based more on negotiation and persuasion than on direct command.

Those multinational enterprises which sell highly culture-bound products cover the whole spectrum from high to low headquarters direction and from high to low standardization of marketing programs. What distinguishes them seems primarily to be the extent of their international experience.

Less experienced firms with highly culture-bound products tend to manage the marketing function in a manner very similar to that of most firms whose products are culture-free or only moderately culture-bound. For example, several U. S. food firms, when they first went to Europe, also practiced high headquarters direction and high standardization of marketing programs, typically through the transfer of domestic marketing strategies. This approach led to marketing failures, however, because it did not take account of significant differences in local market conditions. Most of these firms did not have adequate systems at headquarters for identifying country-to-country differences in market conditions.

Mature multinational enterprises with many decades of experience in selling highly culture-bound products tend to practice low headquarters direction and moderate to low standardization of marketing programs. Over the years, these firms have found that differences in local market conditions require considerable local custom tailoring of marketing programs. Moreover, they have found that the necessary adaptations are made more efficiently at the subsidiary level than at headquarters. The dominant role in marketing decision making is thus shifted to the subsidiary managers. Foreign operations are integrated (1) through the transfer of systems, which educate subsidiary managers and standardize the process of decision making, (2) through the transfer of marketing personnel, and (3) through long periods of acculturation for managers.

A number of normative conclusions may be drawn from these insights into the marketing activities of multinational enterprises in the consumer packaged goods industries.

First, for firms whose products are culture-free, a combination of high headquarters direction and high standardization of marketing programs is effective in integrating multinational operations.

Second, multinational enterprises selling highly culture-bound products need to custom-tailor their marketing programs and, therefore, to give subsidiary managers a great deal of autonomy. Since headquarters direction must be limited, integration is achieved primarily through corporate acculturation, systems transfer, and personnel

transfer. What can be standardized across borders is the <u>process</u>
of marketing program development rather than the actual programs
themselves.

Third, a critical management task in any multinational firm
is to develop a mechanism for systematic analysis of market conditions in all countries. Such analysis can help management avoid
the mistake of standardizing marketing programs when markets are
significantly different. At the same time, systematic cross-border
analysis can help avoid the opportunity cost of excessive custom
tailoring when markets are sufficiently similar to make standardized
programs feasible.

Finally, the long-run competitive strength and flexibility of
any multinational enterprise may be enhanced by developing in
subsidiary managers the competence for making better decisions
and by creating in them attitudes that induce them—without constant
supervision from above—to act in conformity with worldwide corporate
policies. In other words, even firms that can effectively use headquarters direction as the primary integrative device should simultaneously seek to transfer marketing knowledge across borders
through effective planning systems and through training and acculturation of their managers.

Aharoni, Yair. The Foreign Investment Decision Process. Boston:
Harvard University, Graduate School of Business Administration,
Division of Research, 1966.

Alsegg, Robert J. Control Relationships Between American Corporations and Their European Subsidiaries. New York: American
Management Association, Inc., 1971.

_____. "Reorganizaing the International Operation," The Conference
Board Record, December 1971, pp. 52-64.

Andrews, Kenneth R. The Concept of Corporate Strategy. Homewood,
Ill.: Dow Jones-Irwin, Inc., 1971.

Anthony, Robert N. Planning and Control Systems: A Framework for
Analysis. Boston: Harvard University, Graduate School of
Business Administration, Division of Research, 1965.

Aylmer, Richard John. Marketing Decisions in the Multinational
Firm. Doctoral dissertation, Harvard University, Graduate
School of Business Administration, 1968.

_____. "Who Makes Marketing Decisions in the Multinational Firm?"
Journal of Marketing, October 1970, pp. 25-30.

Barlow, E. R. Management of Foreign Manufacturing Subsidiaries.
Boston: Harvard University, Graduate School of Business
Administration, Division of Research, 1953.

Bartels, Robert. "Are Domestic and International Marketing Dissimilar?" Journal of Marketing, July 1968, pp. 56-61.

Berg, Thomas L. Mismarketing. New York: Doubleday & Company,
Inc., 1970.

Britt, Stewart Henderson. "Standardizing Marketing for the International Market," Columbia Journal of World Business, Winter
1974, pp. 39-45.

Brooke, Michael Z., and H. Lee Remmers. The Strategy of Multinational Enterprise. New York: American Elsevier Publishing
Company, Inc., 1970.

Bursk, Edward C., et al. Financial Control of Multinational Opera-
    tions. New York: Financial Executives Research Foundation,
    1971.

Business International. Acquisitions Abroad. New York: Business
    International Corp., 1963.

____. Organizing for European Operations. Geneva: Business
    International, S. A., 1967.

____. Organizing for Worldwide Operations. New York: Business
    International Corp., 1965.

Butler, W. Jack, and John Dearden. "Managing a Worldwide Busi-
    ness," Harvard Business Review, May-June 1965, pp. 93-102.

Buzzell, Robert D. "Can You Standardize Multinational Marketing?"
    Harvard Business Review, November-December 1968, pp. 102-13.

Cateora, Philip R., and John M. Hess. International Marketing,
    rev. ed. Homewood: Richard D. Irwin, Inc., 1971.

Chorafas, Dimitris N. The Communication Barrier in International
    Management. New York: American Management Association,
    Inc., 1969.

Clee, Gilbert H., and Alfred Di Scipio. "Creating a World Enterprise,"
    Harvard Business Review, November-December 1959, pp. 77-89.

Clee, Gilbert H., and Wilbur M. Sachtjen. "Organizing a Worldwide
    Business," Harvard Business Review, November-December 1964,
    pp. 55-67.

Corey, E. Raymond, and Steven H. Star. Organization Strategy:
    A Marketing Approach. Boston: Harvard University, Graduate
    School of Business Administration, Division of Research, 1971.

Dichter, Ernest. "The World Customer," Harvard Business Review,
    July-August 1962, pp. 113-22.

Dunn, S. Watson. "The Case Study Approach in Cross-Cultural
    Research," Journal of Marketing Research, February 1966,
    pp. 26-31.

____, ed. International Handbook of Advertising. New York:
    McGraw-Hill Book Company, 1964.

Dymsza, William A. Multinational Business Strategy. New York: McGraw-Hill Book Company, 1972.

Elinder, Erik. "How International Can Advertising Be?" in S. Watson Dunn, ed., International Handbook of Advertising, pp. 59-71. New York: McGraw-Hill Book Company, 1964.

____. "How International Can European Advertising Be?" Journal of Marketing, April 1965, pp. 7-11.

____. "International Advertisers Must Devise Universal Ads," Advertising Age, November 27, 1961, pp. 91-96.

Fatt, Arthur C. "The Dangers of 'Local' International Advertising," Journal of Marketing, January 1967, pp. 60-62.

Fayerweather, John. "Foreign Operations: A Guide for Top Management," Harvard Business Review, January-February 1957, pp. 127-35.

____. International Business Management: A Conceptual Framework. New York: McGraw-Hill Book Company, 1969.

____. International Marketing. Englewood Cliffs: Prentice-Hall, Inc., 1965.

Fouraker, Lawrence E., and John M. Stopford. "Organizational Structure and the Multinational Strategy," Administrative Science Quarterly, June 1968, pp. 47-64.

Franko, Lawrence G. European Business Strategies in the United States. Geneva: Business International S. A., 1971.

Gabriel, Peter P. The International Transfer of Corporate Skills. Boston: Harvard University, Graduate School of Business Administration, Division of Research, 1967.

Gruber, W. H., and D. G. Marquis. Factors in the Transfer of Technology. Cambridge, Mass.: M. I. T. Press, 1969.

Gruber, W. H., Dileep Mehta, and Raymond Vernon. "The R & D Factor in International Trade and International Investment of United States Industries," Journal of Political Economy, February 1967, pp. 20-37.

General Foods Corporation—International Division (D 1). Boston: Harvard University, Graduate School of Business Administration,

1964. Distributed by Intercollegiate Case Clearing House,
Soldiers Field, Boston: Order No. 9-313-213.

General Foods Corporation–International Division (D 2). Boston:
Harvard University, Graduate School of Business Administration,
1964. Distributed by Intercollegiate Case Clearing House,
Soldiers Field, Boston: Order No. 9-313-214.

Gestetner, David. "Strategy in Managing International Sales,"
Harvard Business Review, September-October 1974, pp. 103-08.

Greene, James, and Michael G. Duerr. Intercompany Transactions
in the Multinational Firm. New York: The Conference Board,
1970.

Hall, Edward T. "The Silent Language in Overseas Business,"
Harvard Business Review, May-June 1960, pp. 87-96.

Heller, Norman. "How Pepsi-Cola Does It in 110 Countries," in
John S. Wright and Jac L. Goldstucker, eds., New Ideas for
Successful Marketing, pp. 694-700. Chicago: American
Marketing Association, 1966.

Hess, John M., and Phillip Catora. International Marketing.
Homewood: Richard D. Irwin, Inc., 1966.

Hildebrandt, H. W. "Communication Barriers Between German
Subsidiaries and Parent American Companies," Michigan
Business Review, July 1973, pp. 6-14.

Holton, Richard. "Marketing Strategy in Development of International
Business," in F. E. Webster, ed., New Directions in Marketing,
pp. 123-30. Chicago: American Marketing Association, 1965.

Hufbauer, G. C. "The Impact of National Characteristics and
Technology on the Commodity Composition of Trade in Manufac-
tured Goods," in Raymond Vernon, ed., The Technology Factor
in International Trade, pp. 145-231. New York: Columbia
University Press, 1970.

Jay, Antony. Management and Machiavelli. New York: Holt,
Rinehart & Winston, 1967.

Keegan, Warren J. "Key Questions in Multinational Marketing
Management," Worldwide P & I Planning, July-August 1970,
pp. 64-70.

_____. Multinational Marketing Management. Cambridge, Mass.: Marketing Science Institute, 1970. (Working Paper.)

_____. Multinational Marketing Management. Englewood Cliffs: Prentice-Hall, Inc., 1974.

_____. "Multinational Product Planning: Strategic Alternatives," Journal of Marketing, January 1969, pp. 58-67.

_____. Scanning the International Business Environment: A Study of the Information Acquisition Process. Doctoral dissertation, Harvard University, Graduate School of Business Administration, 1967.

Knickerbocker, Frederick T. Oligopolistic Reaction and Multinational Enterprise. Boston: Harvard University, Graduate School of Business Administration, Division of Research, 1973.

Kolde, Endel J. International Business Enterprise. Englewood Cliffs: Prentice-Hall, Inc., 1968.

Kuin, Pieter. "The Magic of Multinational Management," Harvard Business Review, November-December 1972, pp. 89-97.

Lawrence, Paul R., and Jay W. Lorsch. Organization and Environment. Boston: Harvard University, Graduate School of Business Administration, Division of Research, 1967.

Lovell, Enid Baird. Managing Foreign-Base Operations. New York: National Industrial Conference Board, 1963.

Mace, Myles L. "The President and International Operations," Harvard Business Review, November-December 1966, pp. 72-84.

_____, and George G. Montgomery, Jr. Management Problems of Corporate Acquisitions. Boston: Harvard University, Graduate School of Business Administration, Division of Research, 1962.

March, James G., and Herbert A. Simon. Organizations. New York: John Wiley & Sons, Inc., 1958.

Martyn, Howie. Multinational Business Management. Lexington, Mass.: Heath Lexington Books, 1970.

Mauriel, John J. "Evaluation and Control of Overseas Operations," Management Accounting, May 1969, pp. 35-39.

Miracle, Gordon E. "International Advertising Principles and
    Strategies," MSU Business Topics, Autumn 1968, pp. 29-36.

_____. Management of International Advertising. Ann Arbor:
    University of Michigan, Bureau of Business Research, 1966.

_____. "Product Characteristics and Marketing Strategy," Journal
    of Marketing, January 1965, pp. 18-24.

Negandhi, Anant R., and Bernard D. Estafen. "A Research Model
    To Determine the Applicability of American Management Know-How
    in Differing Cultures and/or Environments," Academy of Manage-
    ment Journal, December 1965, pp. 309-18.

Newman, William H. "Is Management Exportable?" Columbia Journal
    of World Business, January-February 1970, pp. 7-18.

Parks, F. Newton. "Survival of the European Headquarters," Harvard
    Business Review, March-April 1969, pp. 79-84.

"Percentage of Sales Invested in Advertising in 1967-68," Advertising
    Age, January 25, 1971, pp. 77-78.

Perlmutter, Howard V. "The Tortuous Evolution of the Multinational
    Corporation," Columbia Journal of World Business, January-
    February 1969, pp. 9-18.

Polaroid France (S. A.). Boston: Harvard University, Graduate
    School of Business Administration, 1968. Distributed by
    Intercollegiate Case Clearing House, Soldiers Field, Boston:
    Order No. 9-513-119.

Pryor, Millard H., Jr. "Planning in a Worldwide Business,"
    Harvard Business Review, January-February 1965, pp. 130-39.

Robbins, Sidney M., and Robert B. Stobaugh. Money in the Multi-
    national Enterprise. New York: Basic Books, Inc., 1973.

Robinson, Dwight E. "U. S. Style of Life Invades Europe,"
    Harvard Business Review, September-October 1968, pp. 140-47.

Robinson, Richard D. International Business Management. New York:
    Holt, Rinehart & Winston, 1973.

_____. International Management. New York: Holt, Rinehart &
    Winston, 1967.

Robock, Stefan H., and Kenneth Simmonds. International Business and Multinational Enterprises. Homewood: Richard D. Irwin, Inc., 1973.

Rocour, Jean-Luc. Management of European Corporate Subsidiaries in the United States. Doctoral dissertation, Cornell University, 1963.

Roostal, Ilmar. "Standardization of Advertising for Western Europe," Journal of Marketing, October 1963, pp. 15-20.

Ryans, John A., and James C. Baker, eds. World Marketing, A Multinational Approach. New York: John Wiley & Sons, Inc., 1967.

Ryans, John K., Jr. "Is It Too Soon To Put a Tiger in Every Tank?" Columbia Journal of World Business, March-April 1969, pp. 69-75.

Schollhammer, Hans. "Long-Range Planning in Multinational Firms," Columbia Journal of World Business, September-October 1971, pp. 79-86.

Schwendiman, John Snow. Strategic and Long-Range Planning for the Multinational Corporation. New York: Praeger Publishers, Inc., 1973.

Shapiro, Stanley J. "Comparative Marketing and Economic Development," in George Schwartz, ed., Science in Marketing, pp. 398-429. New York: John Wiley & Sons, Inc., 1965.

Simon, Herbert A. Administrative Behavior, 2d ed. New York: The Free Press, 1965.

Skinner, C. Wickham. "Control in a Multinational Corporation," Worldwide P & I Planning, May-June 1967, pp. 24-32.

Smith, George Albert. Managing Geographically Decentralized Companies. Boston: Harvard University, Graduate School of Business Administration, Division of Research, 1958.

Snyder, Watson, Jr., and Frank B. Gray. The Corporate Marketing Staff: Its Role and Effectiveness in Multi-Division Companies. Cambridge, Mass.: Marketing Science Institute, 1971. (Working Paper.)

Sommers, Montrose, and Jerome Kerman. "Why Products Flourish Here, Fizzle There," Columbia Journal of World Business, March-April 1967, pp. 89-97.

Sorenson, Ralph Z. The Analysis of Competition Between Local and
    International Companies in Two Central American Industries.
    Doctoral dissertation, Harvard University, Graduate School
    of Business Administration, 1967.

_____. Multinational Marketing Leverage, 1st rev. Research
    Proposal, Harvard University, Graduate School of Business
    Administration, 1971.

_____, and Ulrich E. Wiechmann. "How Multinationals View Marketing
    Standardization," Harvard Business Review, May-June 1975,
    pp. 38-45.

Stanley, Alexander O. Organizing for International Operations.
    New York: American Management Association, 1960.

Stobaugh, Robert B., Jr. Product Life Cycle, U. S. Exports, and
    Investment. Doctoral dissertation, Harvard University,
    Graduate School of Business Administration, 1968.

Stopford, John M. Growth and Organizational Change in the Multi-
    national Firm. Doctoral dissertation, Harvard University,
    Graduate School of Business Administration, 1968.

_____, and Louis T. Wells, Jr. Managing the Multinational Enter-
    prise. New York: Basic Books, Inc., 1972.

Streglitz, Harold. Organization Structure of International Companies.
    New York: National Industrial Conference Board, 1965.

Terpstra, Vern. American Marketing in the Common Market. Doctoral
    dissertation, University of Michigan, 1967.

_____. International Marketing. New York: Holt, Rinehart & Winston,
    Inc., 1972.

Unilever Limited. The Anatomy of a Business: Unilever Management
    in Structure and Operation. London: Unilever Ltd., 1962.

_____. Style in Management: The Unilever Experience. London:
    Unilever Ltd., Information Division, 1970.

_____. Unilever's Role as a Multi-national Business. London:
    Unilever Ltd., Information Division, 1972.

United Nations, Department of Economic and Social Affairs. Multi-
    national Corporations in World Development. New York:

United Nations, 1973. U. N. Doc. No. ST/ECA/190; U. N.
Sales No. E. 73. II. A. 11.

Vernon, Raymond. "Future of the Multinational Enterprise, " in
Charles P. Kindleberger, ed. , The International Corporation,
pp. 373-400. Cambridge, Mass.: M. I. T. Press, 1970.

____. "Multinational Enterprise & National Sovereignty, "
Harvard Business Review, March-April 1967, p. 156.

____. Sovereignty at Bay: The Multinational Spread of U. S.
Enterprises. New York: Basic Books, Inc. , 1971.

____, ed. The Technology Factor in International Trade.   New
York: Columbia University Press, 1970.

Ward, James J. The European Approach to U. S. Markets: Product
and Promotion Adaptation by European Multinational Corporations.
New York: Praeger Publishers, Inc. , 1973.

Wells, Louis T. , Jr. Product Innovation and Directions of International Trade. Doctoral dissertation, Harvard University,
Graduate School of Business Administration, 1966.

____. "The Multinational Business Enterprise: What Kind of
International Organization?" in Robert O. Keohane and Joseph
S. Nye, eds. , Transnational Relations and World Politics,
pp. 97-114. Cambridge, Mass.: Harvard University Press,
1972.

Wiechmann, Ulrich E. "Integrating Multinational Marketing Activities, "
Columbia Journal of World Business, Winter 1974, pp. 7-16.

Williams, Charles R. "Regional Management Overseas, "
Harvard Business Review, January-February 1967, pp. 87-91.

Williamson, Oliver E. Corporate Control and Business Behavior.
Englewood Cliffs: Prentice-Hall, Inc. , 1970.

Wind, Yoram, Susan P. Douglas, and Howard V. Perlmutter.
"Guidelines for Developing International Marketing Strategies, "
Journal of Marketing, April 1973, pp. 14-23.

Wrigley, Leonard. Divisional Autonomy and Diversification.
Doctoral dissertation, Harvard University, Graduate School
of Business Administration, 1970.

Yoshino, Michael Yootara. Managing Selected Marketing Functions in International Operations. Doctoral dissertation, Stanford University, 1962.

____. "Toward a Concept of Managerial Control for a World Enterprise, " Michigan Business Review, March 1966, pp. 25-31.

Zenoff, David R. International Business Management. New York: The Macmillan Company, 1971.

ULRICH E. WIECHMANN is Assistant Professor at the Harvard Business School, where he teaches marketing and international management both in the graduate degree program and in executive development programs. He has also taught at INSEAD, France, and is involved in executive education and case research at Keio University, Japan.

He earned his masters' degree at Mannheim University, Germany, and received his doctorate in business administration from the Harvard Business School.

Before joining the Harvard faculty, Professor Wiechmann worked in Germany and in Great Britain in the fields of marketing, shipping, and merchant banking. He has been a member of the Institute of Marketing at Mannheim, Germany, where his work focused on marketing productivity studies and management consulting in both industrial goods and consumer goods companies.

His research activity to date has concentrated on product profitability analysis, distribution systems, sales management, and international business. He has published on such topics as distribution cost analysis, sales force compensation systems, franchising, and multinational marketing.

In addition to his teaching and research activities at the Harvard Business School, Professor Wiechmann serves as a consultant to European and U. S. companies and is actively involved in the design and implementation of company-internal and company-external programs for executive development. He is a faculty associate of Management Analysis Center, Inc., a management consulting firm with offices in the United States and Europe.

**ECONOMIC ANALYSIS AND THE MULTINATIONAL
ENTERPRISE
                                edited by John H. Dunning

THE EUROPEAN APPROACH TO U. S. MARKETS:
Product and Promotion Adaptation by European
Multinational Corporations
                                James J. Ward

FOREIGN DISINVESTMENT BY U. S. MULTI-
NATIONAL CORPORATIONS: With Eight Case
Studies
                                Roger L. Torneden

FOREIGN PRIVATE MANUFACTURING INVESTMENT
AND MULTINATIONAL CORPORATIONS: An
Annotated Bibliography
                                Sanjaya Lall

INTERNATIONAL LABOR AND THE MULTINATIONAL
ENTERPRISE
                                edited by Duane Kujawa, foreword by
                                Raymond Vernon

*MANAGING MULTINATIONAL CORPORATIONS
                                Arvind V. Phatak

MULTINATIONAL CORPORATIONS AND GOVERN-
MENTS: Business-Government Relations in an
International Context
                                edited by Patrick M. Boarman and
                                Hans Schollhammer

*Also available in paperback as a Praeger Special Studies Student
Edition.
**For sale in the United States only.